VALU
ABLE

**[HOW A VALUES-ENABLED
CULTURE CAN INSPIRE YOU
TO SUSTAINABLE PROFIT]**

MIKE JENNINGS

FROM POULTRY FARMER TO ETHICAL BUSINESS CHAMPION

Valuable

Mike Jennings

First published in the United Kingdom in 2018 by Ethical Enterprises, Hampden House, Monument Park, Chalgrove, Oxfordshire OX44 7RW

Copyright © 2018 Mike Jennings

Typeset and designed by Blooberry Design Ltd

British Library Cataloguing-in-Publication Data.

A CIP record for this book is available from the British Library.

ISBN: 978-1-9999040-0-5

Printed in the United Kingdom

Acknowledgements:

With thanks for the help and support I have received in writing this book: From the team at Ricks Café, whose service, coffee and music has always been exemplary and a great backdrop for much of my writing. From the team at Jennings who have been patiently and expectantly awaiting delivery of the finished book about them. From several enthusiasts who have given their time to trawl through drafts of the book for errors, punctuation and illogical arguments. And from Blooberry Design and their editor for pulling the rough manuscript into something a bit more readable, I hope.

Dedication:

To an incredible team without whose tolerance and patience this story could not have happened.

About Valuable:

When everyone knows that being in business is synonymous with being hell-bent on maximising personal income, it takes some courage to write a book that shows the exact opposite is not only possible, but also a cultural trend which is growing fast. This book shows that by putting people first, ie social and environmental responsibility, it is possible to build a financially sustainable business.

Mike explains very clearly how his model works, starting from a set of behavioural Values which are used to unite the team, through a clear statement of Purpose which transcends the need to focus on profit and allows all team members to make decisions.

As team members build their own personal self confidence through this process, so the business as a whole starts to grow and succeed. Doing business for good leads to attracting good customers, good suppliers and good employees. Business then becomes easier, more productive, more adaptable and more profitable. Doing business this way is indeed Valuable.

Contents

Four ways to improve customer service

1   Delegate it to your customers. Let them give feedback, good and bad, early and often.

2   Delegate it to your managers. Build in close monitoring, training and feedback. Have them walk the floor, co-creating with their teams.

3   Use technology. Monitor digital footprints, sales per square foot, visible customer actions.

4   **Create a culture where peers inspire peers, in which each employee acts like a leader, pushing the culture forward. People like us do things like this. People like us, care.**

You've probably guessed that the most **valuable** one, the fourth, is also far and away the most difficult to create. **Culture is a posture that lasts. It's corroded by shortcuts and by inattention, and fed by constant investment and care.**

Big company or small, it doesn't matter. There are government agencies and tiny non-profits that have a culture of care and service. And then there are the rest…

Seth Godin, Author and Entrepreneur

Highlights by Mike Jennings

This book is a description of how a culture such as Seth describes has been created in a small business in Oxfordshire, England.

Profit is not the main motive

Corporate social responsibility is measured
in terms of businesses improving conditions
for their employees, shareholders,
communities, and environment. But moral
responsibility goes further, reflecting
the need for corporations to address
fundamental ethical issues such as inclusion,
dignity, and equality.

Klaus Schwab – Founder and Executive Chairman
of the World Economic Forum

The purpose of a business enterprise is to maximise return to its owners, the Shareholders. That is the economic basis of business, which I learned at economics classes at school, cemented by my Business Studies course at University, and of course it is generally accepted by all. Profit is merely a return on capital employed. I believed it. It makes sense......or does it? What about the human impact.

Even back then for me there were worrying signs. I remember well our case studies, at university, of Slater Walker – the British industrial conglomerate and bank – who were vilified as 'asset strippers'. Their strategy was to buy a business, make the employees redundant, then sell the assets off piecemeal. I remember also 'Tiny' Rowland who was CEO of Lonrho – a huge mining corporation that had extensive operations in Africa – where worker exploitation was common. Both are cases of employee exploitation, justified in many ways economically, but smelling of greed and coming from power.

It has never felt comfortable to me that in the pursuit of profit, humanity is often side-lined. Actually that statement is pretty weak, so I will rephrase. The culture of putting profit ahead of caring for our fellow human beings or our environment (which is the same thing) was and still is an absolute disgrace. We should be ashamed of ourselves.

Greed, selfishness, short-termism. Call it what you want. It is an uncomfortable way to make a living when you are preying on those less fortunate.

This modus operandi has become so pervasive in our Western society that it is simply accepted. How many times have I been told not to take poor behaviour personally? 'It's just business,' they say, as if that makes abuse acceptable. Or they allay blame by claiming, 'It is not illegal,' which seems to absolve them of the moral responsibility for their decisions.

We have normalised abuse in the name of business.

Furthermore this corporate culture that has seeped into politics, bureaucracy and even into the professional arenas. It is a culture of greed where short-term profit is seen as the only objective, and the need to retain power by laying off blame is paramount. When mistakes are called out, the immediate reaction is not to accept responsibility and apologise, but to set brand-damage-control in motion.

Once we realise that this is happening, we see it everywhere.

Perhaps the peak moment so far in this evolving storyline is the current attitude of scapegoating whistle-blowers. People who tell the truth in order to make our society a better place are chastised, even hunted down, with the effect of minimising the likelihood of others following their courageous example. And yet we should be treating these purveyors of honesty as heroes, as long as their honesty is not putting other people in jeopardy.

We tend to assume that the primary duty of directors in the UK, as enshrined in Company Law, is to maximise shareholder value to the exclusion of all else. However, the 2006 Companies Act made it clear that company directors are now required to take into account the interests of other 'stakeholders' in the form of employees, suppliers, customers and the wider community. The intention is to encourage a culture where the wider consequences of decisions are considered.

This has led to a new concept, that of Corporate Social Responsibility (CSR).

Unfortunately tendency to short-termism and personal greed is so pervasive in the corporate culture that the other stakeholders are still ignored, and almost all CSR is inauthentic. It has become a public relations exercise. Companies will confidently display how much they are doing for charity, but still treat stakeholders with contempt.

Even if a corporation sets out with good intentions in terms of CSR, even if the directors are passionately intent on helping, their efforts are doomed to fail because the drive for short-term profit is almost bound to break down any genuine attempt. What starts from the head – a positive desire to do something – never quite reaches the heart of the business. What gets in the way is all the manipulation and Machiavellian politicking that is rife throughout most organisations as people compete for hierarchical status.

One result of this is that brand values are being rinsed out. Marketers will tell you that the purpose of a brand is to sell product. But there is little integrity left in many of the bigger brands, and little trust. As this fact becomes obvious to consumers, so brand integrity diminishes.

A sad consequences of all this contemptuous behaviour is that it has become normal, accepted and expected. It is virtually impossible to fight. Those that do are ostracised. Careers are cut short. The easiest route is to accept the culture, emulate it even, keep your head down, do nothing to rock the boat, and just do as you are told. Thus the culture, down to the human interaction level, is built on power, hierarchy, status and dependency. All this is incredibly damaging both to the human psyche and to the growth prospects of a business. Arguably it is also the cause of much stress in the workplace and thus the birthplace of, or at least the catalyst for, much ill-health. The stress and anxiety generated can lead to or exacerbate heart and lung problems, strokes, depression and higher sensitivity to allergies – with no clear method of dealing with these human conditions in the workplace.

The truth is that it is virtually impossible to break the mould. What I have observed all my life has become so much the norm that we naturally assume it is the only way to do business. Short-term profit is so visible, whereas long-term relationships are hard to define. The metrics we use for success in everything business-related – including business awards – are based on numbers: the highest profit, the fastest-growing sales, the most exports, the greatest number of employees. Rarely is success measured in softer ways, such as happiness, motivation, integrity, trust.

Furthermore any attempt at improving working conditions is likely to be met with suspicion by employees. As consumers, we question the motivation in everything. I recently bought a soft drink that proudly stated in capitals: 'NO ASPARTAME'. My immediate reaction was not 'oh, that's good' but 'what ingredients are they hiding under this headline?'

The art of doing business for the sole benefit of shareholders and directors has made the rest of us suspicious of motives to such an extent that any attempt to offer support to other stakeholders is often dismissed by doubt or ridicule. It takes a strong leader to push through the barriers and really make a difference.

The bigger the business, the harder it is to make cultural changes. Making changes in a large organisation is a bit like trying to steer a supertanker; it takes time, space and patience. It is much easier to steer a small yacht.

Happily, the vast majority of businesses in the UK are small enough to have an owner who also manages the business. According to the UK Office of National Statistics, in 2016, there were 2.5 million businesses registered for VAT or PAYE, and of those over 98 per cent had fewer than 50 employees, and over 90 per cent had fewer than ten employees. In these businesses, the owner can have serious impact. His or her values can be impressed upon the team. The owner can choose to put people first, to have a strong and uniting purpose and a realistic, holistic set of Values which determine the way in which the team is expected to behave.

Putting trust at the heart of the business

That is what this book is all about: a description of a model of running a business which has fairness, honesty, equality and trust at the heart. It is the story of my family business, which has been operating for nearly 100 years with increasing success.

While the model is based on my thoughts, dreams and actions, especially these past ten years, I could not have achieved the success without the willingness and adaptability of an exceptional team. A team, I am proud to say, that just gets better and better.

This is no academic model. This is a real working model in a business which is in the UK top 5 per cent based on employment. The model is predicated on an ethos of authentic leadership rather than management, of trust rather than control, where people are treated as equals and at the same time respected for their diversity.

We have proved beyond doubt that an ethically responsible approach is the route to sustainable, profitable business. As long as shareholders and directors are not greedy, all stakeholders can benefit.

It has not been an easy journey. I have suffered many doubts and listened to, and usually chosen to ignore, many doubters. At the same time, there have been many successes along the way and massive learning. I have learned, for example, that fulfilment as a business owner comes not from metrics – such as ever-higher profits or turnover – but from seeing team members united in a common purpose and so motivated that they behave as though they are volunteers. These successes cannot be measured by standard methods but they can be felt, and that makes them even more real.

I have learned beyond doubt that the source of our expansion is the growth in the self-confidence of each member of the team, and as we grow the business, so the team members benefit as well. It is a mutually beneficial arrangement. Self-confidence leads to innovation, flexibility and willingness to invoke and accept change, all of which are vital in a fast-moving business environment.

The story that follows is a warts-and-all journey of uncertainty, anxiety, trial and error, unexpected outcomes, failures, and eventually the prize of a smoothly running, highly motivated team who share a common purpose and understand behaviour around a set of agreed Values. We have achieved the goal of a team made up of leaders and innovators, all accepting that everyone has a voice and that everyone has life beyond the business.

We are not at the end of this journey, and I guess we never will be as the culture continuously grows and develops. However, it is already clear that the possibly surprising outcome is that the business is more profitable and easier to lead than it has ever been. I hope that in reading this book you may develop the confidence to adopt a similar approach in your own business.

This **Valu**es En**able**d approach is indeed valuable.

CHAPTER ONE

My Journey to Jennings

Learning the professional
and corporate models

**But then they send me away to teach me how to
be sensible, logical, responsible, practical.
And they showed me a world where I could be so
dependable, clinical, intellectual, cynical.**

Supertramp – '*The Logical Song*'

My grandfather was the son of a college servant. His father was Head Porter at Worcester College, Oxford. After the First World War, my grandfather took a risk. He bought six eggs to hatch, and from that beginning he built a business. When it comes down to it, all businesses start with one person with an idea, who is prepared to take a risk. My grandfather was an entrepreneur.

In the mid 1920s, with one son born (my uncle) and one to come (my father), he bought land at Garsington – a village south-east of Oxford – and started to build a poultry farm. Initially selling eggs, during World War II the farm changed to hatching and selling young birds for people to keep in their back yards. The business then reverted to egg sales in the 1950s and prospered until the mid 1970s, when the large supermarkets started to impose their purchasing power on farmers with the threat of buying cheaper, subsidised, eggs from abroad. That was when the business changed again and my father and uncle – forced into searching for alternative uses for their premises or go bankrupt – began to convert farm buildings into workshops. This turned out to be an inspired decision, and we now run a thriving business park of over 100 tenant companies.

As it turns out, that decision also changed my life.

Early life // morals, rebellion and the value of hard work

As a child I had the freedom to roam the fields around us. We lived in quite a big house and I was acutely aware that my friends at school mostly did not. We were also isolated at one end of the village. I had a sense of inequality at an early age, and I was the unequal one! I also had a sense of being isolated emotionally as well as physically. I knew how hard my father worked and how little we saw of him, even though his job was right outside the house. Looking back now, I can see how all these things impacted me in later life.

The business had good years and bad years. In good years my father extended the house; and in the bad, my mother worried about cost savings. I remember once her complaining that my sisters used too much toilet roll! We holidayed with family in Blackpool, ten of us camped out in a three-bedroomed council house. It was a five-hour trip to Blackpool in those days, before the advent of motorways, but it was an adventure.

My mother instilled in me a strong sense of what is right and what is wrong. She made sure I went to church every Sunday. I attended Sunday School. I joined the church choir and I learned to ring the church bells. I was confirmed by the bishop. I went along with it all even though I did not really believe in it. I was a bit of a rebel, and eventually was thrown out of the choir for talking too much.

My father made sure that I was aware that money comes from hard work. As a young boy I used to collect the eggs or feed the chickens. I remember that my sisters and cousins and I were treated with immense fairness in that we were paid for the work we did – the same wages as the employees whose work we took on when they were on holiday.

This combination of respect for Christian values and for the value of hard work has been with me all my life. The rebelliousness in me is still there, too, but somewhat matured.

I think now that this is the essence of enterprise – the ability to think and act differently than the norm.

I owe this quality especially to my grandfather and to my father.

Education // individuality, conformity and achievement

Most of my friends went to the local secondary modern school, but because I passed the 11+ exam I was offered a choice of secondary school. My father asked me which school I would prefer to go to. I was allowed to choose! Even now I look back on that moment as my father showing me that with freedom of choice comes responsibility. I decided – and only I could be responsible for the outcome. I was the only one from my primary school to go to Littlemore Grammar School.

The first few days were frightening and lonely. In my first few years, I grouped with other rebels. Nothing bad, just a few broken windows, nipping to the 'out of bounds' fish and chip shop at lunchtime, and a lot of playing up in the lessons. After all, this was a grammar school and we were expected to behave and learn. Eventually I realised that I needed to knuckle down if I was going to get anywhere. I changed the group I associated with and began to study. I sometimes wonder if that was a detrimental step: choosing conformity over rebelliousness. Fortunately, the rebel in me had not gone away; I had just supressed him for a while.

I scraped three A levels, with low grades, but sufficient to get me to university. I had no idea what I wanted to do, and so drifted into a business degree. In those days – the late 1970s – the courses in Business Administration (DBA) were not good. I was at Bath, a former engineering college. The engineering students I knew at Bath University worked hard – really hard! They knew that one-third of their number would be rejected at the end of the first year. On my course, we did hardly anything. The engineers renamed my DBA course 'Do Bugger All'. Now, I believe, this has all changed.

Conformity or creativity?

Looking back, I wonder whether this is what schooling does for our children: teaches conformity and thereby stifles the creativity which comes from individuality. Entrepreneurs are people who are prepared to take a risk, to do something different. I wonder how many more entrepreneurs we could produce if only we encouraged individuality at school, rather than streamlining everyone into conformity. (I am talking about an entrepreneurial spirit here rather than specifically a business owner. It is, of course, possible – and I think preferable – for employees to behave in an entrepreneurial way, as we shall see later.)

The course is called Bachelor in Business Administration (BBA) and is well respected. The point is that when I graduated, I did not feel that I deserved the qualification; I felt no sense of achievement. I have never used the letters BSc in my title. Perhaps this is my Christian values coming to the fore.

There is no pleasure or credit in something that you have gained without having to work hard for it.

The professional firm

After four years at university I still had no idea what I wanted to do. My father suggested accountancy and I could not think of anything better, so I drifted into it. I trained at a firm in Oxford and actually enjoyed it. I had always loved maths, logic and problem solving so it suited me. Accountancy, after all, is a set of rules that need to be applied.

I remember we used to get boxes of paperwork from our smaller clients. The boxes from Chinese restaurants smelled of sweet and sour sauce, the garages all had oily fingerprints on the invoices. We were able to recognise the client by the smell as their box of records was delivered! We had to produce a set of Accounts (profit-and-loss account and balance sheet) from these incomplete records. I loved the challenge. I learned that accountancy is less of a science, more of an art. The science part is obvious: putting the numbers together, processing the paperwork, and so on. The art comes from the understanding that a set of Accounts is there to tell a story. Every number on the balance sheet, except 'cash in bank', is an estimate. Herein lies the dark side of accountancy. The story you are telling depends on who the recipient of the story is. You can choose to tell the truth or you can choose to manipulate. We were honest brokers at the firm I trained with; later I learned more about this darker art.

I enjoyed meeting the clients. I loved being able to show them a complete set of Accounts and explain it to them, and also to work out how much tax they had to pay and what I could do to minimise it within the law. Some of the clients were fun to be around. Some were more difficult. Some lived in the 1920s! At one client company, the old man (the father who had started the business) kept hold of the petty cash tin in the belief that it gave him some control. This I now know was a clear indicator of our need to hold on to control of something that has been part of our lives for so long. Letting go is not easy. With another client, I remember that the Chairman had his own toilet, which was not for the use of the staff! One client told me about a customer who was very late to pay his bill. After many attempts to get paid, my client eventually sent a photo of a tramp with a scraggly beard saying in a note: 'This is what you have reduced me to. I cannot even afford a razor'. The customer sent a razor blade back in the post – and paid his bill shortly after. It was easy to decide which clients I wanted to work with, if and when I had a choice: the ones who clearly enjoyed their work.

I was articled to the Institute of Chartered Accountants. The coursework was intense, done in the evening and on block release (two to four weeks at a time). On the training courses, I met students working for the large accountancy firms. They seemed to have such a poor existence, doing pure audit work, which in my view was really boring. I could not understand how they could put up with it. One student had been working on the Post Office audit for 11 months and had just been told she would be on it the following year. She was resigned to her fate. She felt she had no choice. Another had been doing a 'wages' audit for three weeks – so tedious! Any audit work we did was all over within two weeks, and the payroll part would never take more than a day.

The accountancy exams were taken in two Parts, the first to be passed before studying for the second. Each Part consisted of five three-hour

The apprentice

Recently I heard a parallel to this story. A young apprentice at a local garage was explaining to me how he loved his job because he got to do a bit of everything at the garage, including interaction with customers. He compared his job to another apprentice he knew who worked for a larger garage group. The other apprentice spent all day servicing only one make of car – repeating the same job, changing the same oil and air filters – and therefore having minimal learning. It is easier for larger firms to treat apprentices as servants, without care for their progression, whereas smaller enterprises can more easily give apprentices real-life experience. It comes down to whether the business owner/apprentice manager cares, and is prepared to put the effort in, or whether the profit motive takes precedence.

Of course, there is another side to this: how motivated the apprentice is. At another garage which specialises in classic cars, the apprentice seemed unable or unwilling to learn, repeating the same mistakes many times. The business owner eventually sent him back to the college. Both the business owner and the employee have a responsibility to each other. You can only teach someone who is prepared to learn and you can only learn from someone who is prepared to teach.

exam papers taken over two-and-a-half days. All five papers had to be passed at the same sitting. I failed my Part Ones first time round.

I had never failed exams before. I had never put any effort into exams before either – that's why I failed! I discovered a renewed respect for the exams. I knuckled down. I studied – not hard but consistently. With that attitude, I passed both Parts. I worked hard for this qualification and while I value it more than my degree, I still do not use the letters – they do not represent who I am, but rather just a part of my journey. I have no need of them.

I loved working with the clients. I worked hard, I had fun and I was learning. But after I qualified I realised that I did not want to continue to work in the profession. It seemed to me that the more interesting work was going on in business. The accountancy profession can be a bit aloof. There is a real danger of professionals thinking themselves above those who create the wealth, and I found increasingly that I did not want to work in that environment. Perhaps the subtle rebel in me was expressing his views. Perhaps I did not like all the rules and regulations that we had to learn and abide by, and make sure our clients conformed to as well. They seemed to get in the way of the real work. There was no excitement for me in making business owners conform.

The corporate world

So I made the transition into business. In 1982, I was accepted as an accountant for an up-and-coming business called Oxford Magnet Technology Ltd. They designed and made the first Nuclear Magnetic Resonance (NMR) body scanners using cryogenics. Oxford remains a world centre for cryogenics.

OMT was a fast-paced business. I was initially one of 30 employees, but one of 300 when I left less than two years later. I learned a lot, especially from my boss, Chris, who was an accountant who had trained while working in the business sector. We complemented one other, but he had built up the wiles that meant he knew how to survive corporate life.

We had to produce monthly accounts within two weeks of the month end and send them to the Group. Chris was determined to get our accounts prepared within a week to beat the others in the Group. We had to make some bold estimates to do this. Mostly it was fine. One month we had a £500k profit, which we knew was a cock-up but could not find the error. Chris suggested we simply adjusted it (hid it) and posted a more regular profit that month, knowing that the reverse entry would sort itself out in the next month or two. Which it did.

In the end, the need to do things to impress others, and dealing with the power-mongering and positioning and back-stabbing, was too much for me. One particular episode that pained me was when I was not given a pay rise I felt I deserved, while the computer manager got a big pay rise. Chris explained that it was because the MD would go home each evening and see the computer manager still at work – apparently ignorant of the fact that he took Friday afternoons off to play golf. It felt unfair.

My life is much simpler than that. I only ever wanted to be honest, work hard, treat people with respect, and in turn be respected. While I did not realise it at the time, my values were being trampled on. All I knew was that it felt uncomfortable.

With hindsight, perhaps what I experienced at OMT is no different from what many people experience every day in the larger organisations they work for. It is far from clear to me why they accept these conditions. Perhaps they feel they have no alternative; perhaps they fear the consequences of leaving; perhaps they thrive in this environment; perhaps this is normal for them.

Later in my working life I have been fortunate to meet many business owners who started their careers working in larger businesses, only to reject that way of life and start their own businesses. These are the courageous people who have rejected conformity and comfort and instead chosen freedom and risk.

My experience at OMT made it clear to me that I was not cut out to work for a large business. Commuting to London in the 1980s where the big money was (the 'loads'a'money' era of Thatcherism so eloquently parodied by Harry Enfield) did not appeal. I was never driven by earning large amounts of money. Being brought up in a big house relative to my friends only made me feel isolated. To do my best and be accepted was my aim. I did not have the confidence to start my own business – anyway, what would I do? Financial expertise did not make me a businessman, I thought. I looked around for a job in a smaller business.

The family business

I joined a local firm of builders. I loved building, and especially the trades. I always have done since I worked with the poultry farm maintenance man during my university holidays; painting, carpentry, plastering, laying tarmac, laying blocks and bricks, mixing concrete. I like to know how things are put together.

I learned about the design of buildings and the progress on site as a building emerges from the ground. We always said, and I expect it is still true today: one-third of the costs in the ground, one-third in the structure, and one third fitting out. The team were immensely proud of their work, and rightly so. The joinery shop produced some great work for individuals and for the Oxford colleges. The bricklayers built an extension at one college which emulated the Victorian master builders. What an achievement that was. All our tradesmen were highly skilled craftsmen. For every contract we could see a building take shape from concept, through design, to construction and use. It requires teamwork where every trade is important to complete the whole. Construction is a great environment to be part of.

I ran the finance department for the company and I was afforded the freedom to set it up how I wanted. I was in charge and my team followed me. I focused on continuous improvement, and provision of good, honest information so that the directors could make informed decisions. Accurate costing is important in building projects, but there is always a balance between time and accuracy. As I have said, accountancy is an art. The aim is to get relevant information for clarity and timely decision-making, not to be precise where that takes too long. One director, I remember, did not like the financial information I provided, and by extension he did not like me. He could no longer hide. Contracts he managed regularly lost money, and my figures showed it. Financial information is honest, if delivered honestly. Clarity and simplicity is the key. Conversely, financial information can be dishonest, and easily used to impact on decision-making. I have heard it said that a financial director has the most influence at Board meetings, and a deviant finance director can manipulate figures, and the stories around the figures, to get what he wants.

In this family company, all the shares had been passed down from father to son, and my boss was the seventh generation. In my opinion, the MD was not cut out to be a builder. He did it because he felt he had no choice. How could he disappoint his ancestors by walking away? He had been set up for this role from childhood. The ties of family businesses can bind us in a negative way. We celebrate long-lasting family businesses, but we often do not see the emotional pressures beneath the surface.

There is no freedom in expectations placed upon you.

The MD was not free to lead his life in the way he wanted. As a result, he had no passion for the business and he would often resort to angry outbursts. The MD liked things to stay the same and he reacted badly to change. I do not think he realised that his outbursts created anxiety amongst his team. Their behaviour changed in order to avoid the outbursts, so in effect he was inadvertently controlling them.

There was a kind of dull acceptance amongst the team which I did not really understand. Why put up with it? Was it because this was also their source of income? Everyone focused on their work and put up with the boss's occasional outbursts, but I knew that I would never run a business in that way. It did not feel healthy.

My situation was different to the other staff. When I joined the company I was already aware that I may leave to work with my father, who had by then started converting poultry units into workshops. I made it clear that I would stay two years, but I gave no guarantees after that. While I did not preconceive this idea, what it meant was that I was one of the few people in the company who was not dependent upon the job because I had already made it clear that I considered it temporary. It meant that I did not fear challenging the MD, and I did so on many occasions, simply by not hiding from the truth. If I thought something was amiss I would say so. I was prepared to take the consequences.

I remember being very blunt when we went through a recession and a few jobs needed to go. The directors agreed with the MD that redundancies should be on a last-in, first-out basis. I was fundamentally against that. I felt that those who were not pulling their weight should go. Everyone knew who these people were, and the message would soon go out that such behaviour would not be tolerated. It is not only about who you make redundant, but the impact it has on the others. To his credit (in my view) the MD agreed with me, despite it

Welcoming challenges

I now know that a very important element of leadership is to welcome the challenges of others. It takes humility to accept a challenge; it bruises the ego; it results in learning (whether that is by seeing the issue from a different perspective or by the resulting thoughtful contemplation strengthening the argument); and it brings about team unity.

costing a lot more in redundancy pay, as these men were often long-standing employees. This sounds a bit brutal, and it was obviously upsetting for those who were made redundant, and their families. It is a truth in business that sometimes factors beyond your control occur, and that may result in necessary cut-backs. This episode was not about making more money. This was about survival.

When I joined I was made aware that the main admin assistant had applied for my job. It was uncomfortable to begin with, but I soon formulated a plan. I told her that I would teach her my job, and I did. This had two benefits. Firstly she came to understand that it was not as easy as she had thought, and she began to accept me as her boss. And secondly I began to realise that my task of giving away my work just allowed me to find more important things to do. I was forced into a position of letting go. I did it in a nurturing way, accepting her mistakes, gently explaining how to do each job, and allowing her to learn at her own pace. I found that I had time to start providing better information to directors, preparing reports they had never had before. Instead of managing people and processes I started to look for opportunities to improve things.

Reducing to the lowest common denominator

One story that comes to mind was of a young apprentice who left after a few months. He explained to me that he could not work with the site agent. He had been told by the site agent to work less hard as he was showing everybody else up. The apprentice didn't even think he was working that hard! He had noticed how the site agent would drink at the local pub on a Friday lunchtime and then allow everyone to leave work early. He also noticed how management accepted this practice, or turned a blind eye. I thought it sad that attitudes like this could affect individuals, and it seemed to me that if this was allowed to continue then the best people would tend to leave, and those that stayed would drop into the same attitude as the existing team.

Working together effectively

Looking back, I realise now that these were important lessons on teams working effectively together. Keep the best people and challenge those who are not pulling their weight. It is so easy to imply that this is an excuse for whipping people into working harder for more profit, but that is not what this is about. This is about having in the team people who are passionate about what they are doing, and work effectively and efficiently because they want to, not because they have to. The more people in your team doing that, the more it encourages the rest. If there are people in your team who are slacking and getting away with it, then others will start to do the same, not because they want to, but because they see it as a lack of fairness. The lesson? – reward commitment. Encourage your people to behave as if they were volunteers and not as if they are slaves. At the same time treat them as volunteers, and not as slaves. In this way it is possible to build a team of individuals who can be proud of themselves, each other and what they have achieved together.

Learning on the job

I learned a lot at the building company, and
I am grateful for the experience. I learned:

- about family businesses, and the way the
employees can look up to the owners with
anxiety more than with respect;

- that the best form of respect is that which
is earned rather than just because of an
executive position, or ownership;

- about passion for the work, the sheer joy
of creating something which is a permanent
reminder of your efforts. With 100 employees,
100 subcontractors and perhaps ten major
contracts and dozens of minor contracts on the
go at any one time, I learned:

- how to keep the accounts and costing simple,
effective and meaningful;

- to deal with professionals such as
bank managers, insurance and pension
advisors, lawyers and commercial agents.
They may be professionals, but they make
mistakes too, I discovered!

Perhaps most importantly, in retrospect, these were
my first lessons in dependency and independency;
the fear of losing a job or income, and the benefits
that can come from letting go of a role rather than
holding on to it.

Transition

I didn't stay for two years. I stayed for eight. But after two years I started taking time off to work for my father. Initially one day a fortnight, then one day a week, then two days a week. One unexpected bonus from having two jobs was that I learned to switch on and switch off almost instantaneously. The knock-on effect was that I could switch off easily on family holidays. Whereas before I used to take a week to wind down, now I could wind down on the journey to the holiday camp (we had young children by then and holidayed on campsites in Brittany). A real bonus.

Inevitably as my father needed more of my time I gave up the job at the building company, and I am proud to say I was replaced by a full-time, qualified accountant!

Meanwhile, back at the farm

While my uncle wound down the poultry side of the business, my father focused on redeveloping the buildings as workshops to let as commercial premises. He needed help, and he valued my financial experience.

Working with my father was not as difficult as I thought it might be. It helped that I had held down a good job and had a professional qualification. He treated me as an equal, for which I was grateful. I knew this stemmed from his own situation. He felt he had no alternative but to work for his father and was trapped through lack of a qualification. He had always encouraged me to:

'Get a trade or a profession, and then come back into the family business if it is right for you and the business'.

I passed this valuable lesson on to my own children, and I am proud to say that they are all doing something that inspires them.

I took the time to observe my father's business methods. He had a gentle approach to the tenants, which I greatly admired. He would often just sit with them and chat. I think he found kindred spirits amongst them. He was respectful and he would always treat them fairly. Some of those early tenants are still with us over 25 years later. Some of them still talk about him fondly, even though he passed away some 20 years ago. I sometimes think that he was simply continuing to behave as a stockman. It makes sense really. If you look after the chickens, they lay the eggs, and if you look after your tenants, they pay the rent.

On the other hand, I did begin to make some changes. His office systems were out of the Ark! But since the business was developed from a farm business, that's not so surprising. I installed central heating into the Business Park office. (When our secretary had previously asked for heating she had been given a cardboard box to put her feet in!) I bought the first office computer, set up a database and began using spreadsheets and computerised accounts systems. And I acquired a cafetière (I like good coffee!).

One of Dad's main tasks was to get planning consent so that he could provide more premises for grow-on space for existing businesses. This was not an easy task at a time when planners were not in favour of employment growth in rural areas. However, with the support of the local councillors, my father was able to convert 32 poultry sheds (4,650 square metres/50,000 square feet) into workshops to house over 30 businesses, employing about 150 mainly local people.

I started changing administration processes, too. My father would visit the tenants every quarter or every month to pick up a cheque for the rent. He then recorded the information in a handwritten ledger book. Even back then it was archaic! While I wanted to visit our tenants, especially the new ones I was bringing into the Park, I did not want every visit to be to pick up a cheque as they would only associate my visits with costing them money. The quarterly collection of rent in advance was also old-fashioned (though it still goes on) and did not help the tenants' cash-flows, as most business people work on a monthly basis. So we changed to monthly payments by standing order – simple and respectful of our tenants' needs. Now I could visit tenants because I wanted to, not because I needed a cheque. This was in the early days when I was just learning about the importance of relationships in business.

I felt the rents we were charging were too low and needed an increase of about 30 per cent to match the market rent for the area. This seemed fair to me, and when we explained the reasons hardly any of the tenants complained when we increased their rents at the next review. They knew the rents were too low. At the time, my father was on the local Board of the now defunct national business support agency called CoSIRA (the Council for Small Businesses in Rural Areas). He phoned them to ask what rent would be reasonable to charge only to find out that they based their rents on what we charged! This was a moment of enlightenment for us. From that point on we set our own rents, based on what we felt was fair, checking occasionally the competition, but never asking anyone for advice.

It was at this time that I had my first experiences with marketing. We had converted buildings at another farm in Garsington, and they did not let easily as it was 1991, a time of recession. The commercial agents generally did not help. We had a networking party for them in one of the units. As far as they were concerned it was free drinks and an excuse to meet friends, but no action came of it. I had just paid for their party! Agents are generally not interested in small units because their commission is based on a percentage of the first year's rent. They make their money from businesses moving. They have little interest in an organisation determined to make it easy for tenants to stay.

Fees and commissions come from transactions, not from stability.

Having said that, we do have a good relationship with a couple of local agents who supply us with just names and phone numbers of prospective tenants while we do the rest. If a tenant moves in, we pay a commission.

Having discounted the agents, we decided to go it alone. I tried a postal mail-shot (before emails) to businesses based in offices in Oxford. Useless. How could I promote empty units to business owners so that the letter arrives on their desk at exactly the time they are thinking of moving? I realised that it cannot be done.

Instead we had to work on recommendation, and that is effective only if you have a good reputation for fairness and trustworthiness. That was something I could build on. Most of our prospective tenants now come from recommendation as a result of our reputation. We have occasionally rewarded people for a recommendation, such as with a case of wine, but we do not promote that. It is a thank-you, not a conditional contract.

My father had suggested I work three days a week initially. I did not appreciate at the time how important this suggestion was for me. It freed me up to start looking around for what else I could do. A leader's job is to search out opportunity, and this gave me the time to do just that. Not that I considered myself a leader back then – I was just doing a job.

The Enterprise Agency movement had just started, and I joined the local agency (Thames Business Advice Centre or TBAC) initially working as a director and funder, and soon after as one of the business advisors. The advisory work, which was mainly meeting and helping people who were thinking of starting or had just started a business, was brilliant. It gave me a fundamental understanding of what makes

Community and Quitefast broadband

As these experiences have had an impact on my thinking, I have become an advocate for people starting their businesses from home and growing them in their local environment as far as possible. Business in this way can create and sustain community. My father used to talk about the community based around farming: the wheelwrights, the blacksmiths, the bakers and butchers. They all worked in their communities, and purchased from and sold to their communities.

Global trade has changed this, and especially the influence of large-scale organisations and fast transportation has allowed for long commuter journeys. The effect has been that local villages have turned into dormitories serving the bigger conurbations, destroying community. However the internet has started to reverse this process. With good internet access, many people can work full time or part time from the rural community in which they live. They remain in their villages and begin to use local services again, thus building community. The ability to promote through the internet has led to a growth in locally grown niche services and products. That is why it is so important to give great internet access to all, and so exasperating when the likes of BT, who clearly have a vested interest in maintaining the old telephony systems, seem to drag their feet. Calling something 'Superfast' when in reality it is inferior to alternatives is just a way of duping your customers. Calling it 'Quitefast,' though, wouldn't be such a great strapline!

an entrepreneur tick; what risks they take and why they do it; the struggles they go through to understand what they have undertaken; the financial upheaval sometimes; dealing with banks and accountants and insurances. Most left good jobs to be free to do their own thing. The truth is that, contrary to what some believe, people do not set up a business because they have nothing else to do. They set up in business because they wish to be free to pursue a passion. How brilliant to be able to assist these people in pursuing their passions! It was a great job, and what I learned here was invaluable in helping me to have empathy for my tenants, a point which became very important to the growth of my own business.

I got involved in many other organisations, too, and met some interesting, inspirational, and locally influential people. I don't think I would have done this if my father had not given me the space to do it. And it has impacted positively both on the business and on me.

Businesslink

One final incident, which is appropriate to mention now, related to the work I did at the time for the local Businesslink.

A little explanation: central government decided that they needed to encourage more people into self-employment and especially for new businesses to grow and employ people, and so they set up and funded a national service called Businesslink. (These have now been decommissioned and the work they did has been taken on by the Local Enterprise Partnerships.) I was asked by the local service to be an advisor, one of 12. I loved the work because I went all round Oxfordshire to visit established businesses (whereas TBAC was exclusively start-ups). One day, the 12 advisors were called in for an assessment, which took all day. The resulting report on me said that I was too gullible – (my word, they put it in far more gentle terms). I still kept the job, but I was gutted. I mentioned this to my father and his response was this:

'It is far better to trust someone first than it is to be suspicious of everyone you meet.'

Boom! In this world of mistrust how brilliant to be prepared and able to extend trust to everyone, and expect that trust to be respected and reciprocated.

Mutual trust

Looking back I now see this event as a seminal moment in my life. With mutual trust, one can begin to build relationships, and that is what our business is all about. Mutual trust comes when you are prepared to extend trust to another person. To do that you have to accept that you make yourself vulnerable. Some people abuse that trust, but in my experience the vast majority respect it. I have attracted around me people who reciprocate my trust in them, and I have had to learn to tolerate or avoid those who take advantage, without judging them. I have also learned to trust more, and to give away power and control in the name of trust. These acts seem counter-intuitive, but the results are what this book is about – loyal customers, a united and motivated team, and steady and sustainable growth. What I would call a truly ethical business, where sustainable profit is an outcome.

CHAPTER TWO

Understanding
Jennings

Developing and implementing
new working methods

Don't just stand there, do something.

Dick Dastardly – *Wacky Races*,
Hanna-Barbera Productions

My father passed away suddenly in 1995. It was a shock. I had worked with him (three days a week) for only three years. I had learned a lot from him, but you cannot easily separate the accountant from the man, and the financial imperative ruled me for some years after his death.

My father was well loved by his tenants, and I knew that I could not let them know of his passing by post. I had to – no, I wanted to – go and see them, at least the 15 or so I knew he was particularly close to. Three of them burst into floods of tears as I explained what had happened. How many commercial landlords would be mourned like this, I wondered, and what a credit to his personable approach to running a business. Doesn't this kind of respect count for more than money?

Suddenly I was in charge. The buck stopped with me. I became responsible to the family shareholders. I had lost the only person with whom I could share what was happening in the business. Anxiety kicked in, and so did the emotional loneliness – that gut feeling when I realised that no one else would be able to understand the joy, the excitement, the little moments; and no one else could empathise with the anxiety, the risks, the uncertainty and the little failures.

Faith and trust // it just feels right

At first I felt the need to focus on growing turnover, profit and dividends. This would surely convince my family shareholders to have faith in me. I kept a constant eye on income and costs.

> ## Jennings Business Mentors:
> ## www.jenningsbusinessmentors.org
>
> Much later, I have come to realise that many business owners share my feeling of loneliness, and I set up a business mentoring service as a way to help others address this and other issues. This remains a unique service in that it is free and our volunteer mentors are all business owners, none being from a corporate, professional or bureaucratic background. The mentor's job is to listen well and to share experiences. Through this reflective and empathetic approach, the client can usually work out his or her own path.

The lessons I had learned from my father – and also from the hundreds of business owners I had met as an advisor and as landlord to our tenants – did not evaporate. I was following my father's lead. Trust was still important to me, as was fairness. I was aware that extending trust to people was an act of personal vulnerability, opening the opportunity for abuse. I knew that if things went wrong I could be accused of being gullible. I did it anyway. It felt right – a natural thing to do.

I considered my competitors. They did not operate in the same way as me – was there something wrong with my methods?

What I was doing seemed so far away from the norm, and yet not only was it working, it just felt so right. The business grew. Profits grew, despite the fact that I was treating everyone with respect, and working from integrity. I was also extending trust to my team. Shortly after my father passed away, Paul joined me as property manager. Two weeks later I left him in charge while I took a family holiday. Many years later he remarked how much it meant to him that I trusted him so readily. That episode marked the beginning of a long working relationship based on trust that endures today. He is now Chief Executive of the business.

Hampden House // pushing the boundaries

The first building projects I managed after my father passed away were small ones: redevelopments or extensions. I was building the confidence to tackle something larger. And as my confidence grew, my self-doubts subsided (they never go away entirely!).

Developing empathy

I felt sure that to develop our business integrity it would be helpful for Paul to become an advisor at TBAC. This would give him a good understanding of what people worry about when starting or thinking of starting a business. It helped him to nurture some empathy for business owners which, in my opinion, has helped elevate him to become one of the top property managers in Oxfordshire. Importantly he has developed this approach in helping newer team members attain the same kind of empathy which is so vital in the way we operate the business.

In 1998 I began the largest construction project we had ever undertaken. It worked well. Then in 2000, I experienced the second seminal moment, where I had built up the courage to follow my intuition (remember the first seminal moment was accepting that gullibility is not all bad). I made a decision which was, to an outsider, very risky, and different from what we had done before. I knew it was the right thing to do.

I decided to build an office building: Hampden House. (John Hampden was a prominent parliamentarian who had been mortally wounded in 1643 at the Civil War's Battle of Chalgrove Field, which is nearby. Had he not been killed, it is said he may well have been Britain's first Prime Minister.)

Before then, everything had been manufacturing and warehousing units. Not only that:

- this would be the first speculative build we had done – all others had tenants lined up in advance;
- it would be a serviced office (one where we would manage the building and all the services and the tenants would pay an all-inclusive licence fee);
- this would be the first purpose-built, serviced office in Oxfordshire;
- this would be the only one with large offices.

And on top of all of that, this building would cost twice as much as the previous largest building that I constructed two years earlier.

I remember my uncle (and he was not the only one) doubting my sanity. 'Are you sure you are doing the right thing?'

'Yes,' I surprised myself by responding confidently, and to his credit he backed off and allowed me to get on with it.

Entrepreneurs

Truly entrepreneurial people do not follow what has gone before but rather choose to follow their intuition or their heart. They reflect on their past experiences and they assess what customers may want or need now and in the future. The aim is not so much to maximise profit, but to follow a passion, to try something new, to aim higher. What on the surface is just a person getting on with his or her work, underneath is an emotional journey of assessing risk, having faith and believing in yourself.

I just knew that this new building would be the catalyst to raise what was an industrial estate into a business park. I also knew that I could not possibly 'control' the build process. It was too big. So I worked from trust.

Building the team // it's all about relationships

Instead of a competitive tender process, I selected the builder for the job, and also the foreman. I based my decision on their previous work and the fact that I trusted them. The price was less important (but not unimportant, I hasten to add). I got all the professionals together and explained that we were all here to make a profit, not to fight with each other. This turned out to be an inspired comment because it took away fear of blame if anything went wrong. The only arguments (not really) were over whose turn it was to buy the bacon sandwiches at the fortnightly early-morning meetings! Bear in mind that I had worked in the building contracting industry, and seen at first hand the disagreements between architects, engineers, surveyors, contract managers and foremen, each trying to win a bit more money for their company, or to allay blame to another for something that had gone wrong. I did not want that on this project.

The foreman planned a few weeks ahead and asked for my opinion on everything – and I mean everything – down to the colours, the style of door, the windows, the door handles, the number and position of electrical sockets. I chose the subcontractors I trusted and enlisted their opinion on everything from alarm systems and telephony to 'who turns the lights out' and 'who locks the door'. These things sound straightforward now, but I was trailblazing, and it felt good – and mostly we got it right. The rebel in me was given room to play, and I did, focusing on what I knew our tenants would want. That was my expertise. From design to completion, this building was both emotionally enthralling and draining. I loved it, to the extent that every building project that followed became insignificant. They gave me little opportunity to aim higher, but rather just to do more of the same, and to me they were boring.

Building relationships with customers is one thing, but the other side of that process is building relationships with providers (suppliers, contractors and professionals). I selected for this project contractors and subcontractors who not only did the job but were not afraid to offer their opinion even if I hadn't asked for it. They added to the process. How much they charged was less relevant than their ability to use their experience, know-how and enthusiasm to enhance the project. And this has been how we have worked with our providers ever since. It is as simple as asking for and valuing their opinion, trusting them to do their best work for us.

In the build process, each person in the team had their own trade/ professional experience. My experience meant that I knew the tenants' needs even before they had become tenants. I made sure there was plenty of open space, kitchens and toilets, and wide corridors. I decided how much parking was required. I decided that the sockets for each room would be on a separate circuit so no tenant could blow the circuits of another. I decided that we would have open lawn space to the front, and a pond. I decided that internal walls would be all blockwork to minimise noise and to minimise damage. I decided that all services would be in the ceiling (lights, smoke alarms, air conditioning, etc.) or in the skirting boards (electricity, telecoms), so that the walls would be clean and easy to redecorate when a tenant vacated.

Obviously I worried about the cost and whether we would fill the space. The ultimate mark of a successful build is that it attracts tenants and is profitable. I needn't have worried; it has been incredibly successful. Of course, I made one or two mistakes. But this project, like all projects, was never about perfection.

> **Trying to be perfect exerts too much pressure. It was and is always about doing my best work, with a great team. Mistakes are for learning. We all make mistakes, and the wisest people learn rather than condemn.**

Bringing in the right tenants // enthusiasm and prejudice

While the building would uplift the estate into a business park, that did not mean we would not continue to respect the niche manufacturing tenants. It would be a mixed-use park, open for all.

I remember showing round a couple of prospective tenants in sharp suits. I was proudly talking about all the things that excited me about the building – but probably boring them because there was actually no need to 'sell', I only needed to 'enthuse'. There is a difference.

The best salesmen are enthusiasts for what they sell, and I am proud to say that my team now work in the same way. People buy enthusiasm.

These two guys, having spent about half an hour looking round, asked: 'Is there an alternative route to get to this property without driving past all the industrial units?' I was stunned! I realised they were talking about the people not the buildings. My response was something like: 'This is a mixed-use business park where we all work together. If this is not for you, then you need to look elsewhere.' Shortly after, they walked out. I knew in that moment that I could not work with such prejudice, and I was glad to see them go. Even though I was keen to let the premises at that time, I would never want to be that desperate. One of our competitors could deal with them.

Leases, licences and legalese // transparency, simplicity and honesty

I needed to arrange contractual documentation for the new tenants. At that time, all other tenants were on long-term leases of six or more years. For Hampden House I needed a short-term licence, which is a different, simpler document. I acquired copies from some of our competitors. What I saw dismayed me. Why were they so long, written in 'legal English' (not the same as 'easy-to-read English' or, as I call it, 'English') and in very small print? Did anyone read them? The licensees had only to give one month's notice to vacate. There was no need for a long and complicated agreement. It seemed too heavy-handed. I determined to write my own licence, in plain understandable English, and to make it fit on one side of A4.

I read the licences from our competitors and stripped the documents down to basics. Then I rewrote them in plain English and sent the resultant one-page document to my solicitor. He offered me a job! He has a dry sense of humour. That document became our licence contract, and it is still the same now – 15 years later. It is a simple annual licence which is easy for prospective tenants to read and understand. The tenants stay if they are happy and if their business is doing well. They leave if they have to, and circumstances for leaving vary from moving back to their home or outgrowing the premises to a change of ownership. Rarely does anyone leave to go to a similar-sized office with a nearby competitor. I don't think that has ever happened. That would be a sign that something is wrong. The licence gives the tenant the flexibility to move on if they need to. It gives them independence from us as their landlord, and that is the crucial point that I learned about business owners when I was adviser for TBAC – that business owners value their independence.

A few years later I realised that we could do the same for our longer-term leaseholder tenants. Instead of a 36-page lease, perhaps I could reduce the size of that contract document as well? The catalyst for this came when one prospective tenant returned our lease to us with the spelling mistakes crossed out in red ink. There were quite a lot of mistakes, though mostly minor. This was a word-processed document. No-one else had noticed, including me. That implied that everyone – well over a hundred previous tenants – had signed it without reading it. What kind of madness is this and what does that tell us about how much of business activity, especially amongst small businesses, works on trust, despite the appearance of control through the use of professional documentation.

I decided to rewrite the lease. It took just a day. I deleted every clause that was clearly only put in there to 'control'.

'To preserve unobstructed and undefeated all rights of light and other easements appertaining to the demised premises in any way and at all times to afford to the Landlord such facilities and assistance as may enable the Landlord to prevent the acquisition by anyone of any right of light or other easement over the demised premises or any part thereof.'

Letting leashold premises

The process for letting leasehold premises to prospective tenants used to be as follows:

We showed the prospective tenant round, enthused with them (can't help ourselves!), told them honestly about the competition, offered to let them chat to any of our existing tenants – everything to make them feel comfortable and safe, and assure them that they could trust us.

When they agreed the terms and were ready to move in, we gave them the key and explained that the lease would follow. Our solicitor did not approve of the tenant having the key before they had signed the lease. (Apparently that gives them rights to which they are not entitled until they have signed.) Even back then we were much more tenant-aware than most commercial premises operators are today. This is not how it would work if an agent were involved.

Then, after carefully and honestly building a relationship of trust, the tenant had a large, and very legal, contract document arrive in the post: the lease that no one read. This was a kind of 'sign this or else' moment. It undermined, however subtly, the relationship we had so carefully nurtured. The lease left a flavour that we did not trust the tenant. I did not blame our solicitor, indeed our lease was already one of the shortest. But nonetheless, this had to change.

I got rid of many clauses that were mindless (unless you had a legal mind) and clearly added as a result of an incident that had been decided in the courts in the past.

'Not to do or permit or suffer to be done on the demised premises anything which may cause any insurance of the demised premises or any other part of the Estate effected by the Landlord to become vitiated or whereby the premium payable under any such insurance is liable to be increased and to indemnify the Landlord against any such increased or additional premium which may be payable by reason of any act or default on the part of or caused or permitted by the Tenant in particular (but without prejudice to the generality of the foregoing) the Tenant shall not bring or cause or permit to be brought on or into the demised premises any item which an insurance company would class as 'hazardous goods' without first obtaining the written consent of the insurance company or companies concerned and paying any additional premium resulting therefrom'.

Hard work isn't it? All it needed was:

'To comply with any requirements of any insurance company relating to the Premises or the Park in general.'

I also decided to make the lease valid for just three years. This had the advantage of making the leases below the limits for the new rules on Stamp Duty and Land Registry (avoiding unnecessary costs for the tenant). For us a lease renewal is effectively a rent review.

Furthermore, I felt it right to allow the tenant the freedom to vacate if they wanted to. I added a break clause effected only by the tenant, where they could vacate at any time, giving us three months' notice – fair warning so that we could find a replacement tenant.

The lease is now just four pages long, written in plain English. We give a copy to the prospective tenant ourselves, and we keep the whole process in-house. This is simpler and more efficient. It enhances the relationship, builds trust, and makes our customers feel safe. They can

> ## Bargaining power
>
> In order to grant the tenant security beyond three years our leases comply with sections 24–28 of the Landlord and Tenant Act 1959 which give a tenant a right to renew the lease. Many landlords use a Court Order to exclude this provision of the Act, so that at the end of a lease the tenant has to vacate. The landlord does not necessarily want that to happen, but it gives the landlord a better bargaining position – meaning more power.

stay as long as they want and they can vacate if they need to. Now we know that our tenants remain with us because they want to, not because they are trapped by a lease they cannot get out of.

In effect, I had thrown away our power to exert control over our tenants by extending my trust to them, and giving them the freedom to decide to stay or leave at will, all the for benefit of building relationships based on trust and loyalty.

Tend to your customers' needs // don't copy others, lead the way

This is the now-familiar story of rejecting the norms where they do not fit what you need or what you feel your customers need. So many people take the easy route of simply doing what everyone else does.

In my view, blindly copying someone else is lazy. Coming up with something new based on your assessment of what customers need, is the entrepreneurial way. It is a thoughtful process available to anyone, not just managers or directors.

I choose trust over protection

As far as I am aware no other commercial landlord operates in this way. Initially that worried me, but now I know that what we do works and it works well, and I do not worry about our competitors any more. Crucially I do not think I would have done this if we had a good working relationship with commercial agents, and if we did not have an amenable, long-standing, long-suffering and commercially savvy solicitor who treats me as an equal and who I am pleased to say is still working with us. I say this because the professionals are so often entrenched in the established and accepted methods of finding tenants for commercial property. They have a duty to 'protect' their clients from tenants who may seek to take advantage, and their profession is so full of scare stories that they operate this duty with gusto. My experience was and still is that I could trust prospective tenants. I did not need a professional to tell me otherwise, and for their methods to cause damage to any relationship I was nurturing.

It also helped that I made a decision when first taking on staff never to employ anyone who had experience in the commercial property industry, no surveyors, and no one trained as a commercial agent. A common mistake is believing that property-letting is focused on the property. Instead, at Jennings, we took on people who we believed would build relationships in line with my belief that while our financial investment is in the buildings, our authentic investment is in the people who work from the buildings. Treat them well, with courtesy and respect, and everything else will fall into place. If anyone, even contractors, mistreated any of my tenants, I would be quick to remind them who paid their wages! (By which I mean to remind (not threaten!) them that the money comes from the tenants.)

It is better to trust // strong and lasting relationships

During this process I was acutely aware that I was extending trust to people, both customers and providers. I remembered the 'gullible' jibe, but remembered more my father's wise words.

I guess it is a truism that we tend to notice more those who hurt us rather than those who respond to the courtesy or trust we extend to them.

There were plenty of times when people took advantage of my good nature. When that happened, I felt hurt and I felt others judging me for my mistakes (even if they weren't). My reaction, and perhaps here I am more unusual than many, was to extend my trust even more. Extending trust is a way to build long-term relationships and, looking back, I think I got it about right. Where people did take advantage, it was never a disaster. You tend to think of yourself as a bit of a fool, but you soon get over that. Instead of blaming myself, I learned. I learned that there are some people that you just do not want around. I learned that if you behave in a certain way, then you tend to attract and retain around you people who have the same attributes. Most importantly I learned that if I got it wrong sometimes, then I had to accept members of my team getting it wrong sometimes too.

It turns out that the ability to trust others is a great and underestimated strength, and the first step to building strong and lasting relationships which ultimately underpin all sustainable businesses.

Just ask

I remember one great example of trust where we needed to expand our café and build it into a 'Costa'-style outlet. There was only one place it could be, and we had a tenant who had been firmly established in those premises for over 20 years. I decided to simply ask if he would move. To the surprise of my fellow director, the tenant first agreed to move, then asked why, and then what alternative premises we had in mind for him. In that order. It was that easy because of the relationship of trust that we had built up over those years. It is not easy to put a financial value on that way of operating, but for ease of operations it takes some beating!

CHAPTER THREE

Building
Confidence

———

Discovering the essence of trust and
the importance of failure

You're braver than you believe, and stronger than you seem, and smarter than you think.

Christopher Robin – *Pooh's Grand Adventure*

Something else my father said to me was: 'Listen to your advisors, but make your own decisions'. I meet so many who blindly follow the advice of so-called experts. Sometimes, and especially in larger organisations, this is a cover for failure or error. 'I got the best advice' may be an excuse in a large organisation, a way to lay off the blame, but in a small business we have to stand or fall by our own decisions. Mistakes cost.

Advisors give their opinion, but do not always have to face the consequences.

As business owners we learn to follow our intuition, our 'gut-feel', which comes from a variety of sources, including experience and talking to other business owners, consultants or advisors. I would particularly advocate meeting and talking to other business owners, where you can share real experiences around the anxieties and frustrations, and also the joy and excitement of working for yourself.

Learning to be yourself and to make your own decisions, sometimes against advisors' expert opinion, is about building your self-confidence. Business owners build self-confidence as they become more comfortable in their business. The act of choosing to run your own business is an act of independence, the consequence of which is that your confidence grows. But this does not come easily. Business owners have their doubts and uncertainties just as much as anyone else. Over time, as we learn to think for ourselves, we make decisions, take risks, and deal with uncertainty. Then, as we reflect on successes and learn from mistakes, we grow in confidence. We learn to accept self-doubt, seeing it not as a problem to overcome, but as a friend that is invaluable in helping us to assess risk.

This is a journey that all business owners must take, but few talk about it. People often make the assumption that we are all strong willed and, because we find it difficult to talk about our doubts and fears, that impression sticks. Sometimes we feel we need to give the impression that we are tough, bottling up our uncertainties in the belief that they may make us vulnerable. Giving the impression of certainty, on the other hand, makes us look strong. It took me many years to realise that the truth is the exact opposite.

Being prepared to be open and honest about our doubts and anxieties comes from a position of great personal strength and self-belief.

Being in charge // rejecting control and perfection in favour of trust, respect and kindness

Control is something of an illusion. If you control as much as you can in order to feel in charge, you will soon discover that people don't necessarily do what you expect them to do. A customer does not pay, a supplier fails to deliver, a contractor offers substandard work, a professional gives unsound advice, a team member thinks they know better or takes short cuts.

It is hard enough to run a business without having to put up with other people's intransigence and therefore it is frustrating when this happens because it has a knock-on effect on our business, and it is easy to take it personally. Then there is the question of how to respond: should we be angry or critical? Who do we blame?

When these things happened to me I tended initially to let it go, blaming myself, thinking I did not give good enough instructions. I tried to understand why it had happened and to give people a second chance. But that always felt like a weak response. Surely I should expect the right behaviour and challenge people when that did not happen? But I came to understand that my instinctive choice was on the right path.

There is a tendency when things do not go to plan to want to exert ever more control in a search for perfection. That process inevitably leads to micro-management. It is stressful, destructive and ultimately can lead to damaged health. I was beginning to follow that path and people noticed that I was going grey – in complexion, not hair (yet). The need to show continuingly increasing profits and turnover put me on a toxic treadmill that I did not know how to get off.

What felt right (giving a second, and sometimes a third or fourth chance) seemed to come across as weak-minded. What felt strong minded (to exert more control) was stressful for me, and I was not prepared to do that.

I therefore tried my best, as my father had done, to extend trust to tenants and prospective tenants. I made every effort to play fair, by seeking to understand them and accommodate their needs. Where I could take advantage for short-term gain, I deliberately held back because taking advantage just felt like the wrong thing to do. I treated tenants with courtesy and respect and I worked from integrity – my word was my bond. I did this upfront, without expectation of return, not when I knew I could trust a tenant, but before I knew I could trust them. I wanted my tenants to know they were safe with me, that I would never take advantage of them. That is why, for example, I used to give new tenants a key so that they could start immediately, rather than waiting for a lease to be signed. My uncle used to say, 'treat people as you would expect them to treat you', which I now know comes from the Sermon on the Mount in the Bible, and it seemed so natural to do just that.

The only time I did start to feel undermined was when a tenant says they will sort something out and then do nothing about it and refuse to communicate. But one tenant's lack of integrity did not mean that I had to respond by controlling all tenants. And people only rarely took advantage of the trust I offered. For the most part:

- tenants did deliver on their promises;

- tenants responded in kind;

- when I extended trust I was respected for it;

- when I was generous, it was appreciated;

- people did not take advantage;

- we were able to build lasting, trusting relationships, as illustrated in the examples on pages 55-56

What began to dawn on me was that if you start with trust and then give people the space to work it out for themselves, by not being attached to their response rather than controlling it, then in time they will usually come to accept, reciprocate and then emulate. And if not, then you just have to let your customers go.

As an experienced business mentor, I now accept that the uncertainties and self-doubts that I experienced are normal for anyone running a small business and, in the early years, are a major reason why business owners hold back from growing a business. Two particularly difficult uncertainties focus around taking on your first employee and making your first move into premises. Doubts are often compounded by experiences (either your own experiences or stories heard from acquaintances) of employees, or landlords, who take advantage. Concerns about the power of a landlord and the complexity of employment law make it easier not to bother. If trust and integrity were more commonplace in business, these anxieties would reduce and surely small businesses would be more likely to grow.

The way to address this problem is to talk about it to another person who understands about self-doubt: another business owner. That is what mentoring is about.

Positive re-evaluation of debt: letting go

One tenant was poor at paying rent, but could never come up with a credible reason. A lot of time and energy was wasted chasing him up until finally – when he owed about four months' rent – one of his neighbours on the Park called me one Saturday evening to say that this chap looked as though he was clearing out! Sure enough, I arrived to find him just finishing emptying his unit of terracotta pots into a large white van. I decided to follow him. After all, the pots belonged to my company in lieu of unpaid rent, so I followed him for about an hour up the motorway towards Birmingham.

Then it slowly dawned on me that I was wasting my time. Okay, I had lost the rent. But the upside was I had got rid of an unreliable tenant without any hassle, and he had cleared up the unit. It would be cheaper, quicker and easier to re-let the unit rather than chase the loss. What I did was focus on the future and see it as an opportunity to find a good tenant. The weakness would have been to pursue a lost cause; the strength to make a decision to let it go. Our attachment to the desire to make everyone behave in the way we expect is a distraction.

Honesty in the face of financial difficulty — cementing the relationship

One day I received a call from a tenant asking for a two-month rent holiday to help him solve his temporary cash-flow difficulties. He had already replaced his company car with a cheaper one and reduced his salary; his staff had agreed a temporary salary reduction; and he had contacted his suppliers who had all agreed to give him longer to pay. To me, this showed he was a man of integrity, who was trusted by his team and his suppliers, so I was happy to oblige. Not only did he pay the back rent a few months later, but it cemented our working relationship.

If I had followed the management-style protocol, I'd have stuck to the rule that reduced rents are unacceptable. That would have been weak. The strength comes from having faith in your fellow humans, a belief that they generally have integrity.

Of course, it is not just what you do but how you do it that is important. In this case, I could have drawn up a contract — I will do that as long as you do this — or agreed with reluctance. What I actually did was discuss the problem and show empathy and support, knowing that for most people it is very difficult to ask for our generosity. This empathetic approach can sometimes lead to us offering more than the person has asked for.

Ending a long-term relationship // grace, fairness
and the external marketing department

Tenants under most leases are expected to leave premises in the same condition as they found them. Someone has to assess any dilapidations, and the assessment can cause a breakdown in the relationship.

I regularly hear of business owners being charged 'unfair' dilapidations when they vacate. Stories like this breed anxiety among business owners that their landlord might do the same; they also stick to certain landlords or agents, who become known amongst the business community. Not only that, but such stories hold back businesses that might otherwise grow if it were not for the uncertainty associated with signing a lease.

One particular tenant who had outgrown our Park had an awful experience with their next landlords, who charged them huge dilapidations at the end of their five-year lease. It resulted in a court case. Then the same ex-tenant leased land at another business park and built their own premises, only to be stitched up by the land owner for excessive and increasing service charges.

On our Business Parks, we try to assess dilapidations in a fair way. I was uncomfortable charging large dilapidations; it seemed unfair on the tenant. But then we ended up paying some quite large sums on property repairs. Obviously, we needed to strike a balance and in order to achieve this, we took other action – such as in the example on page 58 – to minimise the potential for damage to occur in the first place. The aim was to control the process – thereby limiting the potential for damage – so that we did not have to control the tenant.

Nowadays we rarely charge for dilapidations. We generally ask a leaving tenant to tidy the unit, sweep up after them, and then pay a small contribution to the redecoration costs. Most tenants are very comfortable with the fair deal on vacating and know that the majority of landlords are much tougher. For example, when I popped in to wish John, who had been with us for over 25 years, a happy retirement, I found him and his wife quite happily painting the walls. My team had requested that he simply tidied up and repainted, ready for the next tenant.

Recurrent problems ... simple solutions

In the past, we had some tenants who caused big problems with the units. For example, oil leaking on to a concrete floor was a major issue because the only solution is to dig up and replace the concrete, which is expensive and disruptive. To avoid having to deal with a particularly difficult client problem, we took the simple solution of stopping accepting enquiries from car mechanics and plastic mould-injecting firms.

Another issue was to do with damage to the walls. True, the thin, soft, clinker block walls of the poultry units were easy to damage but in some cases we were left with repair bills of a full year's rent! We rarely charged this on to outgoing tenants as it did not seem right. But something had to be done, so we went through a process of converting all 32 'sheds' into proper business units, with decent insulation, higher roofs and, crucially, concrete block walls that are much harder to damage.

It seems such a short-sighted approach to take advantage of people just because you can. It is a dishonourable profession that acquiesces to these practices that stem from greed masquerading as 'just business'. Controlling the process around dilapidations allows us to be free to trust our tenants, and then to marvel at the way most of them respond as they appreciate what we have done for them. And because the relationship is not over when a tenant leaves, their positive experience of us as landlords can become an addition to our external marketing efforts. Teaching this to my team encourages them to be fair to a vacating tenant, rather than taking advantage of them.

Respect for our tenants

Our job as landlords is to make the tenants feel comfortable so that they can worry less about the premises, and focus on building their business. If their business grows, then so does ours. We do this by treating them with respect, as equals, and never doing anything to take advantage of them. We want them to feel that we value them.

Alterations // accommodating our tenants' needs

Another contentious area in commercial property is related to alterations to premises. I met recently with a local bank manager whose office premises were owned by a national insurance and pensions company (as many are), and then let through an agent. He told me how, within a few months of moving in, his broadband lease line developed an intermittent fault. As it ran under the building and was impossible to access, they needed to lay a new cable over the roof.

The landlord's agents said he would have to pay a fee and any legal costs. The solicitors demanded they sign a 'deed for alteration'. Overall it cost the bank over £5,000 just to get permission to lay a cable. To me, this exercise of the landlord's power over the tenant is a form of abuse – unnecessary, undermining of relationship, and yet not uncommon.

In contrast, where our tenants want to adapt the unit we almost always agree, subject to the fact that we may need them to reverse the changes when they leave. There is no fuss. While some other landlords make these alterations very difficult, we try to accommodate our tenants' needs, but we expect them to be fair to us by agreeing to pay the costs of removing the alterations, if requested.

Again, this process again did not happen overnight. Feeling uncomfortable blocking the tenants' needs on the one hand, but aware that being accommodating may cause future problems, we decided to agree but with minor provisos. Instantly comfortable with the process, we grew into confidence that this is the right way to behave. It has its rewards.

The more we trusted our tenants in this way, the more we were able to see the rewards of our trust, in terms of loyalty, honesty and trust reciprocated.

Rewards for respect and fairness // loyalty, confidence and growth

1   When tenants are struggling financially, they invariably tend to make sure they can pay the rent first, not because they have to or for fear they may get thrown out, but because they want to. This may seem hard to believe, but it is the truth. Most people respect the fact that they have been treated well.

2   Almost all our tenants live in the local community. We do not want them to say anything negative about us. On the contrary, we hope

they will all recommend us as landlords, as that is what helps our business grow.

3   When existing tenants are looking to grow their business, they will come to us first because they actively want to stay with us. Obviously this is partly for their own convenience, but the point is that we do not put up any factors that could give them a reason to leave. As they grow, so we grow. Almost all of our newer, larger units have been built to accommodate the growth of existing tenants. This 'organic growth' is steady and financially sustainable and I believe is far more socially and environmentally sustainable than 'inward investment' which is promoted by the public sector.

4   When tenants are struggling they come and talk to us for options. It may be a simple rent holiday, or we may allow subletting, or we may suggest they take a smaller unit. We once had a case where two tenants swapped units. One was growing, and the other was reducing in size. We managed the transfer at no cost to the tenants. In fact, we gave them both one month free of rent to help smooth the process, and to show that we empathised with the fact that moving meant they weren't earning. Our reward was that they both stayed with us as customers for many years. I cannot stress enough the importance of communication, and that comes so much easier when there is trust between both parties.

5   Perhaps the best example was when I needed the tenants' help to support a planning application to have open fields allocated for development within the Local Plan. Three tenants volunteered to accompany me to the Planning Inquiry to explain that they needed expansion space for their future plans. I remember the Planning Policy Officer telling one of the tenants (Chris) that his staff were unskilled, and that he could easily pick up unskilled workers in a move to Didcot. He was furious. How dare they criticise his staff! What did they know about his staff and their skills? The Planning Policy Officer had made the mistake of assuming that a relatively

low-paid worker is unskilled. It was quite a moment, and shocked both the Planning Policy Officer and the Inspector with the ferocity of his loyalty to his team. We need more business owners like Chris to step up and show their belief in their staff.

I am not sure if it is possible to put a metric to all this good naturedness. It seemed at the time to me a holistic way of doing business where you take into account your customers' needs rather than treating them as a route to more profit. Certainly there has been less stress when customers are friendly, and less stress meant we had more time for developing the business. Growth has happened because we have treated our customers as equals. I did not know that would work when I started out doing this. There is no metric, just a sense that it works and a slow build-up of confidence.

Understanding // sensual awareness, fun and support

It is essential to build up a good understanding of your tenants and their needs – sometimes better than their own. Steve, a long-standing tenant, came to see me one day saying he needed more space. He was surprised when I said, 'I know'! But, as I explained, 'That's my job.' I had already considered another unit for him. 'It is a bit bigger than you want, but we can offer you a lower rent until you fully expand into the space.'

I had been brought up on a poultry farm, remember? I could walk into any poultry unit and within 10 seconds I could tell if anything was wrong – by sight, smell and sound. It is not so different with businesses. I could tell that Steve was squashed into his old unit, and that his business was both robust and expanding. I could tell from the sights and sounds, and also from knowledge of his past through talking to him regularly.

Another tenant, Dave, ran a business despite having had throat cancer and being unable to speak. I admired Dave immensely for running his engineering business by fax (before emails). One day he was at the back of his unit, and spotted me. He beckoned me over and then ran back into his unit. Seconds later, and before I had taken more than a couple of steps in his direction, he returned holding up a sign that said 'F*** Off', then ran back in giggling (still a child even though he was in his late 40s at the time). It was at moments like this that I knew I had the respect and trust of my tenants. They feel at ease.

Dave was concerned about petty crime on the Park. He knew it was the local lads because he had caught them one day, and given them – well let's just say 'a bit of a talking to'. Dave lived in the local village. Later he started a village youth football club in order to give the lads something better to do. It was a no-brainer for us to sponsor the club. This kind of positive action – which comes from empathy and kindness rather than blame and retribution – are worthy of our support.

People before profit // authentic social enterprise

We were beginning to achieve one of our aims: to create an environment where people feel at home.

I was running a business where we put people before profit. However, I did not yet have the confidence to broadcast the fact; that came later. I still was anxious about what other people would think, unsure whether my behaviour could even be called a method. Were we morphing a for-profit business into a social enterprise if we did not put profit first? Was I confident that this behaviour actually results in higher profits because it induces loyalty from customers? In any event I could only work this way, and I justified decisions that may result in short-term loss by my belief that we would profit in the long term.

Applying the lessons // attitude and impact

While the context of this chapter has of necessity been related to my own commercial property business, this does not mean that the lessons cannot be transferred to all other businesses. Tenants are just customers or clients. Admittedly they are generally long-term, regular customers, but almost all businesses have repeat custom. Our attitude to our customers has a huge impact on whether or not they return for more. And for most small enterprises, growth comes from repeat business or recommendation.

If your customers come to you because you are the cheapest, then it may be worth reconsidering your model. The race to the bottom does no one any good. Don't aspire to be the cheapest, aspire to be the best. My objective was always to do the 'right thing', recognising much later that this process has elevated us to be one of the best commercial landlords. We are not the biggest; we do not have the most up-to-date premises; and we do not have the best location. However, I do think that we have the best, most committed property team, that we treat our tenants better than anyone else, and I could even boast that there is not a single tenant or past tenant who would not sing our praises. That alone would be enough for me, but in addition to that I suspect we have the best retention of tenants, the least empty property, and the perhaps the best profit as a percentage of turnover.

CHAPTER FOUR

The Jennings **Team**

Inspiring your team towards
new goals beyond profit

If you hire people just because they can do a job, they'll work for your money. But if you hire people who believe what you believe, they'll work for you with blood and sweat and tears.

Simon Sinek — author and motivational speaker

While I was working on building trust with my tenants, I had yet to consider how to work with my own team. When we took on staff I was so timid about having to do appraisals that I suggested they all report to Paul. Much later I found out that Paul also was uncomfortable with it, but he just got on with it.

Staff in all business enterprises work under a contractual obligation. They do the work they are told to do, and you, the business owner, pay their wages. It is a simple enough arrangement.

Arguably this arrangement has developed from the industrial age, where processes drive the production line. Processes can work well for the businesses, but the repetitiveness is soul-destroying for the employees. It is a control dynamic, favouring a management approach and fostering dependency.

A dynamic environment demands innovation
// trust and anxiety

As we become a more service-orientated economy – and an economy based on micro-businesses and niche manufacturing – it is apparent that it is preferable to expect staff to think for themselves so that they can adapt as appropriate. In a dynamic business environment, where constant change means that processes quickly go out of date, we really need staff to be innovative. This means that as business owners we must create an environment in which this dynamic is encouraged.

This necessitates a move away from control and towards trust.

The real question is – how do we do that?

We were already developing a holistic approach towards tenants based on fairness, respect, equality and trust. Could we do the same for members of the team? What if instead of being bounded by the limitations of a contract, we could show that we were grateful for their time and effort?

There is a different relationship with staff than with customers: a daily interaction that is more personal. There are also potential contractual difficulties. No matter what is said or done, the 'elephant in the room' is that the boss pays the wages. Staff members are likely to do what the boss says, or what they think will please the boss, in order to improve their chance for advancement. Furthermore, the boss intuitively knows about this behaviour pattern. Extending trust to staff is therefore more fraught with difficulties than extending trust to customers. There is more need for balance, more awareness around favouritism, more varied perception of fairness. It is too easy for there to be suspicions around who is giving and who is taking.

I did not want the politicking and shifting for position that I had seen in the corporate world to occur in my own small business. I was worried that it could happen and, even worse, fearful because I had no idea how I would handle it.

Subtle problems in a loyal team // noticing and understanding

By the time Hampden House was built in 2001, we had a team of eight people, including myself and Paul, four of whom managed Hampden House. We were a commercial property company, with no one experienced in letting commercial property. To me, this was a big bonus in that the team was not held back by any experience that put the buildings ahead of the tenants, and also it meant there was no inbuilt hierarchy based on relevant qualifications. However, it did not necessarily mean that the staff put the tenants first.

In general, I had a loyal and trusting team. Paul took his lead from me and my behaviour, and the team took their lead from both of us. That is how it was. However, that did not mean everything was smooth. There were behaviours that I was uncomfortable with, but they were subtle rather than outrageous.

- There were hints of perfectionism, leading to judgement of others.
- There was some arrogance, based on the perceived power that we have as landlords over the tenants.
- There was too much use of rules as authority, rather than trying to understand why a rule had been broken.
- There was not enough ownership, for example, thinking an empty office was someone else's job to sort out.

Worse than the existence of these traits in my staff, I had some of them too – I just did not know it.

I had always tried, in every decision, to consider the needs of the tenants, working from a perspective of empathy, and I had made the assumption that the team would behave in the same way as I did. When they did not, it undermined the holistic approach we were trying to foster, to the point that tenants would notice and sometimes comment.

At that time I was still suffering from doubt about my methods. I had put my customers first, trying new ideas and techniques. Sometimes I failed, but at least I was trying. But at that time I felt that my team did not really understand me or where I was coming from. I felt that I was a poor businessman, especially when my failed ideas lost money. And I felt judged. And I had no idea what to do about it.

Seeking to understand // safety, freedom and equality

As the team grew, I realised that while they liked working with me, they could not see what I could see; they could not feel what I could feel. A business is fundamentally about building relationships, and you build relationships by establishing trust, and you establish trust by the way you behave. At the core was a clear empathy with my tenants which comes from an understanding of the feelings and emotions around risk-taking. I like the concept of seeking to understand rather than being understood which comes from the Prayer of St Francis of Assisi overleaf. Seeking to understand puts the onus clearly on trying to work out why someone behaves in a certain way, rather than criticising or condemning their behaviour.

There were three key areas which I needed my team to be clear about.

Safety For a tenant, the lease is a contract with inbuilt instability. Tenants expect that there will be contractual problems in the future. Rent reviews, lease ends and dilapidations clauses create uncertainty. I considered it my job to make my tenants feel safe and I needed to make my team understand this.

Independence I was acutely aware that every person who runs a business has a strong sense of their own independence. That is one of the main reasons why people set up their own business: to be free to make their own decisions. I made sure that I did nothing to take their independence away from the tenants; on the contrary, I did what I could to honour it (for example, the four-page lease gives our tenants the freedom to stay as long as they want, and the freedom to leave at short notice).

Equality I was also aware of the strong need for equality, especially in our environment where the landlord is assumed to have power over the tenant. It was not enough just to change the lease to give the power away. A sense of equality had to be encompassed in our behaviour,

The Prayer of St Francis –
The Peace Prayer

Lord, make me an instrument of Your peace;

Where there is hatred, let me sow love;
Where there is injury, pardon;
Where there is error, the truth;
Where there is doubt, the faith;
Where there is despair, hope;
Where there is darkness, light;
And where there is sadness, joy.
Grant that I may not so much seek
to be consoled, as to console.
To be understood, as to understand;
To be loved as to love.
For it is in giving that we receive.
It is in pardoning that we are pardoned.
And it is in dying that we are born to eternal life.

and we had to lead on that. For example, I noticed the difference between how I treated tenants and how other team members did the job. I knew that as a landlord I had to be kind, generous and caring. This meant, for example, that for rent review meetings I would drop in and see if the tenant was available for a chat over coffee. I would never book an appointment – that seemed so cold and controlling. Being 'professional' in this way detracts from building relationships.

It takes time to build a strong working relationship with others, and it takes no time at all to damage that relationship. It was always my objective to allow tenants to leave if they wanted or needed to, but do nothing at all to give them a reason to leave. That is why we set up a strapline of 'A home for your business'. We want tenants, and their staff, to feel at home when they come to work. That meant the whole team had to treat them as family, not as a person subject to a contractual obligation.

The line of power and how to use it // fairness

Basically this means being kind to your customers. Exert your power over them where necessary for the good of all, but never exert your power for self-serving reasons.

Some issues are difficult to assess. Where do you draw the line when customers abuse your good nature? If a tenant is making a mess outside his unit, at what point do we clamp down on his behaviour? For me, at the first conversation we have to try to understand, and then explain our point of view. Perhaps the mess is temporary and the tenant felt he had no alternative, in which case he should have informed us. Perhaps he had no consideration of other Park users, in which case he needs to be told the impact of his actions. If there is no change in attitude, and no action taken to improve the situation, then at some point we have to use our power as landlord for the sake of all users and also for the sake of fairness.

This line of power is very important. Use it irresponsibly and you break down the relationship. Use it sparingly, in the right way, and in full explanation of why you are using it, and you gain respect and can build relationships.

I have learned that each person can assess where this line lies. I have also learned to accept that the line is in a different place for each person so that it is impractical to set rules. A team member will often have a better understanding than me of where the line should be drawn, especially if they have built a good relationship with the tenant. The line is a concept rather than a definitive and we will see later on how our Values give us a platform for staff to establish where this line of power exists.

Rules create dependency // we want to encourage mutual trust

In this example, by the way, the easy route would be to create a rule that the tenant cannot spill out of his unit. Our method is deliberately more relaxed than that – we ask the tenants to 'keep the place tidy'. This allows them to spill out temporarily, if necessary, accepting that there is uncertainty in business and there may be a need.

Once you set a rule:

- you give permission for your team to exert control, and that undermines relationships;
- you create a little bit of fear, and often it is not necessary to do that;
- you encourage those who do not like rules (like me, for example) to break the rule.

Rules and regulations control, create dependency, and disable our ability to think for ourselves. Far better, but far harder, to create a general understanding and allow the team to deal with each issue as it arises.

Inherent problems with working without rules // empathy, curiosity and care

But this flexibility of approach has its problems and I knew that I had to re-educate my team to my way of thinking in order to bring them with me. To do that, I had to understand their point of view.

The established and corporate methods in business are what people understand. Sadly, the practices are usually based on the competitive, power-based, masculine business practices. There are rules and you follow them – they give you the security that you know what is expected, which is especially true of new people coming into the team. This is why I had already decided not to employ anyone with experience in the commercial property industry, so that they would not bring expected behaviours with them.

For example, as a boss, I could be flexible in how generous I was to an incoming tenant. I was always comfortable in offering a month or two rent free, or building a step increase in the rent where that better suited the tenant's cash-flow situation. I could base my decision on empathy, curiosity and care, and it might be different for different tenants. It is easy for the boss to give away income like this, but much harder for an employee, who could be accused of wasting company money.

I was not sure how I could get my team to behave in the same way that I could. The main problem, I realised, was me. I needed to find a way to communicate better. And if I did not get the team fully on board, then they would hold back the potential growth of the business. In order to do that, I needed first to fully understand what I was trying to do. What was basically gut feel and intuition needed to be set down on paper for all to see. And in doing this, I faced my biggest fears of all: what would people think of me, and what if it all went horribly wrong.

My innovative tenants

Every business has a story, and they are all interesting, if you care to take an interest.

There was the sausage manufacturer who was the first to sell sausages on the internet (this was always my example of innovation, which is not necessarily technical but just about thinking of new ways to do things).

Or the cookie manufacturer who discovered that it was not possible to make decent cookies in the USA and so he continues to make the dough in the UK and fly it out to New York and Las Vegas. He considers Chalgrove (where the Park is based) to be the 'world centre for cookie dough technology'.

Or the tenant who 3D prints 3D printing machines, which is an interesting iterative approach and still makes me smile.

Or the tenant who was passing on his business of 20 employees to his grandson, and his grandson's beautifully simple concern that he would be taking on the responsibility for 20 mortgages.

I wanted to be different // strengthening my resolve

I had by then started a network group of business-park managers. They rarely talked about their tenants, whereas I talked about my tenants all the time. I was, and am, proud of their achievements.

I could never understand why other business-park managers rely so much on professionals who generally ignore the humanity of a business relationship. Some business-park managers seemed to have an underlying sense of superiority and I came to realise that this was usually unconscious, probably unwanted, and certainly exacerbated by the behaviour of tenants and others. Other managers followed the normal route of using professionals to get premises let, not even thinking there could be an alternative.

Meeting other business-park owners did not warp me back to their way of running a business. On the contrary it made me stronger in my resolve to continue what we were doing.

I wanted my business to build on what we had already achieved.

- Do more of it, not less.
- Develop relationships further, not go backwards.
- Build community, not undermine it.
- Be united by our actions, not divided.

Relinquishing control // leading the way forward

I realise now that there comes a point in all growing businesses where the owner has no alternative but to delegate to his or her team. Not to do so would prevent growth. There are two ways to do this.

1   To manage: This leads to job demarcation, task-focused appraisals, hierarchy and reward based on metrics.

2 To lead: Trust your team and allow them to develop relationships with your customers.

The first option comes from fear and the second comes from love. These options are opposites, and in your business you will need to decide which method you want to adopt. In practice, most people use a combination of both, depending on the team member in question. I chose to focus solely on the latter method as being much more natural to my way of working.

The starting point for this would be to build a team that shared a similar pattern of behaviours. The following chapters describe how we did it.

CHAPTER FIVE

The Courage to
Move Forward

Implementing the principle of
abundance and abandoning control

Until one is committed, there is hesitancy, the chance to draw back. Concerning all acts of initiative (and creation), there is one elementary truth that ignorance of which kills countless ideas and splendid plans: that the moment one definitely commits oneself, then Providence moves too. All sorts of things occur to help one that would never otherwise have occurred. A whole stream of events issues from the decision, raising in one's favor all manner of unforeseen incidents and meetings and material assistance, which no man could have dreamed would have come his way. Whatever you can do, or dream you can do, begin it. Boldness has genius, power, and magic in it. Begin it now.

Johann Wolfgang von Goethe –
German writer and statesman

One person I could talk to about all of this was my coach. Carlos is a leadership coach and had an interesting background where childhood trauma (abandonment) took him on a life journey, learning from Buddhism and gaining a grounded understanding of people, emotions and the spiritual nature of life. We used to take three-hour early morning walks. He got me thinking from my heart rather than from my head – not an easy job as I had started my business life as an accountant! He explained that the heart has a brain, and so does the stomach. Love comes from the heart and fear is recognised first from the stomach. These two basic emotions are the basis of all emotions.

We use our heads to analyse, our hearts to do what is right, and our gut to assess risk. I learned to use all three, and not just the first.

I remember clearly the first time someone sent me a business email and signed it off with 'love', rather than the usual 'regards'. 'Love' is heartfelt, 'regards' is soulless. I do that now and especially with my team, or I may use the slightly toned down 'hugs' or simply 'x'. How easy it is to simply follow the crowd with email sign-offs, without recognising the significance of words. My thanks to fellow business-owner Stuart for prompting me to do something I should have started years before.

In business we tend to think in terms of a fear-based approach. That word may be too extreme for some, but perhaps we can relate to words and phrases such as power, competition, control, managing, directing, hierarchy, roles, climbing the ladder, ego. We have all experienced the negative side of these terms.

My approach was already much more a love-based approach – again, perhaps more accessible and descriptive words would be trust, equality, humility, kindness, thoughtfulness, openness, caring, supporting, nurturing, believing in others, collaborating, accommodating. Not words normally associated with business!

In short, business seems to be about what one can *take*, but why should it not be about what one can *give*?

We are told that business by default is about making as much money as possible, but why can it not be about personal fulfilment? Business often seems to be self-serving, but why can it not be used to serve others? In my view the greatest achievements for all of us are discovered when we serve. To serve is to be fulfilled. This takes us back to the Prayer of St Francis (see page **70**).

I needed to build a team of givers, who could naturally express kindness and care to others, so that I could trust them in the way they treated our tenants. I needed to focus my attention on the team, and help them to be better at building trusting relationships so that we could better serve our tenants, and through that process we would become financially sustainable, and also enjoy working together as a team. And I include both Paul and myself in that description. We are both still and forever on that learning journey.

Poverty or abundance // clearing out, taking opportunities and motivation

Carlos talked to me about the difference between a poverty consciousness and an abundance consciousness. In business, we tend to think from a perspective of wanting more – my initial focus on turnover and profit is a good example. Or we focus on winning – wanting to be better or bigger than anyone else. This comes from a poverty mind-set; that we just do not have enough.

A much easier and more holistic way to work is from the perspective that there is plenty for everyone. Once you take this on board it transforms the way you work. I see this everywhere, and not just with owners of businesses, but also with their teams.

A poverty mind-set builds attachment: the need to keep hold of tasks granted to you, material things we collect, building personal wealth, and maintaining an existing income stream.

An abundance mind-set allows you to be free of unnecessary burdens and to focus on what is important: the present and the future.

In business it takes courage to turn down work from a difficult client, especially the first time. When a business owner refuses a customer, she is working from abundance. 'I do not need nor want your business'. This is a moment when we recognise and accept the importance of relationships in business over the perceived need to make more money. I have spoken to many business owners about this aspect of business: the moment when they turned down their first client. Emotionally it is a very difficult thing to do, because we fear what others may think of us – it just does not feel right to turn away business. And yet they report that when they do dismiss a client it feels like a weight has been lifted. A single client can occupy not only your active working day, but also your headspace – continuously. These clients tend to be demanding, expecting you to jump to their desires, and actually they work from the financially controlling perspective that you need their business, that you are dependent on them. When you recognise that you don't need them cluttering up your headspace, that is a leap for independence, and it feels good.

It is a bit like having a good clear-out. The tenant I mentioned earlier who moved to smaller premises so that we could build a café took the opportunity to clear out masses of 'stuff' he had collected 'in case it comes in useful'. He later reported how cathartic that exercise was. Most of the 'stuff' was unnecessary.

Where I used to worry about empty premises (no tenant = no income), I stopped worrying, choosing to believe instead that the right person would come along. This put my mind at ease, and that meant I did not have to take on the first potential tenant who came along. It is subtle and it took a long time to let go of the worry, but it is significant, at least it was for me. I still care that all of our premises are let, but I don't worry any more. I worry if the team do not care, but they do, so no worries there – for now.

Of course, at an individual level we are far better off in life if we learn to let go of roles so that another person can take them on.

My coach used to say that knowledge is ours so that we can give it to someone else, not hoard it and/or sell it. There are masses of amazing stories in the Jennings team alone where this can be seen in action. Learn a role, master it, revamp it in your own style, then teach someone else. The freedom you get from letting go of roles allows plenty of time to discover the next thing to do, on the proviso, of course, that you are motivated to do it. This process of Opportunities, not Roles (see The Principles, below) can work for everyone in every business. A business that does not follow this process quickly gets bogged down.

Mirroring // Karma, freedom and emotional intelligence

It is a universal law that people, in general, will mirror back to you the way you treat them.

It is called Karma. In business, we try to buck this principle by using control – a member of your team is paid to do your bidding. Therefore it is acceptable and, of course it feeds your ego, to instruct them what to do. The reality is that by limiting their efforts to doing only what they are told, you are encouraging your staff to make you do all the work. They will simply emulate your methods rather than think for themselves. They will fear making mistakes in case they get blamed. Where there is a problem, they will not make a decision, but ask you what to do. Where you think you are in control of your team, in reality they are controlling you. This is the Karmic effect.

This all became apparent to me in a flash moment when I answered a question from team member Sarah, and she responded: 'Mike, you know everything!' I was devastated. While it stroked my ego, which we all enjoy, I was concerned how she could ever think that! It is definitely not true. Did it mean that she felt she did not need to think, as I could do the thinking for her? Her off-the-cuff remark led me to re-evaluate my behaviour.

It is all about a cycle of control and dependency. I can control a staff member if I make the assumption that they are dependent on me for their salary, which in turn holds them in their dependency. In certain roles, this makes sense, and speed and efficiency can be enhanced by someone who has experience of a particular set of tasks. Some staff feel comfortable with the sameness of their work. Control is therefore not bad all the time, but as a technique in business it can be very damaging.

For the majority, it is better to lead people by trusting them. To do that, it is useful to have some parameters around their behaviours, and some sense of a common purpose which acts as a motivator.

Trusting your team, it turns out, is a brilliant way to set them free to just get on with the tasks in hand, deal with issues as they arise, come up with all sorts of ideas and generally I found they could do a better job than I could. And that frees up the business for growth. I had to behave in such a way that team members would be confident enough to mirror my behaviour.

It turns out that the way you treat your team will reflect in the way your team treat your customers.

Mirroring also works, as I have said before, when you are generous and kind to others. Mostly they appreciate it and a relationship can grow. Occasionally they do not appreciate it, and may even start to abuse your good nature. Then the questions arise:

1   How can you tell they are not appreciative?

2   What are you going to do about it, if anything?

I had to find a way to embrace all of those concepts at Jennings.

Carlos suggested that we start by establishing Values for the business and build a team around a shared set of Values. I did not know what that meant and what issues may arise but went along with the suggestion. I had no other plan. It is no coincidence that the Values are all love-based Values. They are from the heart and they are about building relationships.

Once we did this, there was no going back.

Time to take a deep breath, and go for it.

Emotional Intelligence

Fortunately my wife is highly emotionally aware and that meant that I could check with her some of the things that happened at work, and some of the things Carlos said. This ability to reflect with her has been priceless and helped slow down the whizzing in my brain as I tried to assimilate all these concepts and apply them. She would hear my stories in a completely non-analytical way, working from other senses and intuitively understanding the meaning behind the words. She has taught me by example to do the same.

I began to recognise that behind every person there is a story, built up from our childhood and experiences as we grow. Taking the time to understand our fellow workers and treating them as human beings is the only way to build deep connection, and deep connection turns a group of people into a team.

CHAPTER SIX

Introducing
Values

———

Exploring why it is important to
have a statement of Values

All it takes is faith and trust.

J.M. Barrie – *Peter Pan*

And so it was that Paul and Carlos and I set aside two days to decide on our Values so that we could apply these to the business. We thought two days would give us sufficient time for what, in retrospect, turned out to be an exercise which changed everything.

We settled into a nearby hotel, armed with pencils, paper and drums! We took several deep breaths, and then started talking. We considered many deep questions about the business, such as:

- What is important to us?
- What motivates us?
- What is fulfilling in what we do?
- Why are we even running a business; for whose benefit and how do they benefit?
- How do we want to behave in the future, and how do we want others to behave towards us?
- Can we put a framework round all of the above?

Of course we did not have answers to these questions. We talked around these subjects, waiting for the mist to lift. And what a lot of mist there is. It is far easier to focus on profit!

If I'm honest, this was quite an uncomfortable process for me. We mulled over (I was going to say 'we reviewed', but this was not a technical discussion, it was wide ranging and very non-specific) how we were already operating and focused in on some of our behaviours which I have already mentioned. Why did we behave in some ways that may be considered to be detrimental to the short-term profit of

Coming from the heart

Values come from the heart, and Carlos knew that we had to stay working from the heart. The problem is that we kept over-thinking, using our heads. To get us back to the heart, Carlos had two techniques. One was to stop the conversation, and he squashed all three of us into an alcove where we were nose to nose for a couple of minutes. Pretty uncomfortable, but it gave us a feeling of space again when we went back to the table. It enabled the transition from head thinking to heart thinking. The other method he used was drumming. We bashed out rhythms for a few minutes to bring us back to the beat of our hearts and the tempo of our bodies. Somehow that process closed down the analysis-based thinking that comes from the head and opened up the emotional processes and feelings that come from the heart (though other hotel guests were somewhat bemused).

the business? We knew that our basis for operations with our tenants came primarily from integrity and from really caring about our customers. It also came from an empathetic understanding of their needs. After all in any business, one major objective is to provide what your customers need, and so you have to understand what those needs are. We were also aware that we were in the business for the long term and not for short-term profit maximisation. And we knew that we had the support of my family shareholders. It followed that for us building relationships with our tenants was both a business objective and also a comfortable and less stressful way to go about our daily working lives. We consider our tenants to be our friends, and we have no intention of taking advantage of them. At the same time, while we did not want them to take advantage of us, we were not prepared to control them to prevent it.

Over the two days we came up with a set of Values which reflected quite well what we were already doing, how we were already behaving and what would be aspirational behaviour for our team, and we further defined them through the use of straplines to ensure that our meanings would be clear. These Values remain with us today. We may not have entirely achieved these objectives, but we are trying our best.

- **Openness and Honesty** – for the sake of minimising the fears and anxieties associated with renting premises.

- **Accommodating** – for the sake of making people feel at home.

- **Commitment** – for the sake of delivering a service that exceeds expectation.

- **Fairness** – for the sake of establishing loyalty and trust.

- **Courtesy** – for the sake of creating an environment where people feel valued.

- **Trust** – for the sake of enabling relationships to grow.

There is a kind of circular progression in our Values that makes sense because everything starts and ends with trust. The Values can work independently of each other, and they can work together for better impact and for better understanding. For example, our commitment to provide a service that exceeds expectation is part of the reason that we are accommodating and courteous.

All of the Values lead to building relationships based on mutual trust.

Values are not rules governing exactly what each person does in a given situation. They are guidelines providing a foundation for behaviour. So each person interprets them in a slightly different way. No one is right or wrong, but everyone has the ability to lead in enhancing how the Values operate in practice.

People before profit // what really motivates us?

Having worked for some years with these Values I have come to realise that they are a behavioural foundation for an ethical culture for all businesses where a moral code of conduct is recognised to have a higher purpose than the base intent of maximising profit at all costs.

This is a foundation for a culture that really does put people before profit, and can be applied to all businesses if the intent is there to do it.

Of course, this does not mean that profit is not important; there has to be balance. There has to be sufficient give for the other person to feel they are cared about, but not so much as to bankrupt our own business. With experience, and by focusing on fairness, balance can be found.

And let's be really clear here, having an ability to build long-term relationships, and not do anything to damage those relationships, is good for business. It is much harder to win a new customer than to retain an existing customer. Furthermore customers who become fans are much more likely to recommend your service.

It makes good commercial sense to work from the basis of building relationships.

And let's also be really clear here that I am not advocating that business shouldn't make a profit. What I am saying is that profit should be an outcome, not an objective. An outcome of treating people properly, an outcome of building relationships. For an authentic business, the profit you make is not that important – it is what you do with that profit that is the mark of who you are. For more about this see Chapter 9.

And finally when reading through the Values, you will notice that they relate specifically to a commercial property company, because that is the environment in which we have developed their use. In my opinion, they can just as easily be applied to any company where there is a desire to build long-term relationships with customers, providers and within the team. If you own a small business you may like to consider how these Values could work for you.

CHAPTER SEVEN

The
Values

Outlining the Values through which
we grow our business

**If you don't stick to your values
when they are being tested,
they're not values: they're hobbies.**

Jon Stewart – television host, writer, comedian

Let's look at each of the Values in a little more detail so we fully understand how to apply them in the workplace. While we have defined the Values by associating the issues with the commercial property business, be aware that all the Values can be transferred to any other field of business.

VALUE 1: **Openness and Honesty** – for the sake of minimising the fears and anxieties associated with renting premises

VALUE 2: **Accommodating** – for the sake of making people feel at home

VALUE 3: **Commitment** – for the sake of delivering a service which exceeds expectation

VALUE 4: **Fairness** – for the sake of establishing loyalty and trust

VALUE 5: **Courtesy** – for the sake of creating an environment where people feel valued

VALUE 6: **Trust** – for the sake of enabling relationships to grow

VALUE 1: Openness and Honesty – for the sake of minimising the fears and anxieties associated with renting premises

One of the issues that we recognised very early on, and as we took on more staff, was how we could get the team members to relate to business owners (our customers) in the same way that we did.

Initially I expected the team to emulate my example, but I realised that they could not, simply because they do not run a business. There is a special emotional connection between people who run businesses. It comes from an understanding of the emotional journey; the excitement and also the frustrations; the freedom to make decisions and the self-doubt that accompanies decision-making; the risks and fear of failure and the euphoria of even minor successes such as an order won. People think that business owners are strong, commercially driven, and have deep pockets. Some people think it is acceptable to take advantage of them. Well my view is that business owners have a lot more to put up with than most. Many business owners put on a veneer of strength to mask their uncertainties, worries and anxieties. They have an especially difficult time with commercial landlords, and so for us it was even more important that we treat them with respect and as equals. We needed our team to recognise that without our customers we do not have a business, and then none of us would have a job.

I particularly like the strapline that applies to the Value of Openness and Honesty: *'For the sake of minimising the anxieties and fears associated with renting premises'* is a clear and direct statement to the team that our tenants, and especially prospective tenants, do have fears and anxieties around leasing premises, even if they don't show it. To some in our team at the time we introduced the Values, that would have been a revelation.

In the commercial property world, negotiation with a tenant is usually done from a perspective of competitiveness in the (mistaken) belief that the tenant is strong and has deep pockets. Negotiations can be tough and stressful, leaving both parties exhausted and sometimes feeling they have lost a battle. We choose not to operate in that way and this Value helps team members to understand how to build collaborative relationships rather than compete.

Being honest (telling the truth) and being open (not hiding anything relevant) helps dissipate fears and anxieties, in our case related to renting premises.

When people know they have been given 'warts and all' they know they have everything they need to make a considered decision.

Pinning it with the strapline tells a story to our team – prospective tenants are usually anxious about taking on a lease. In signing a lease, a tenant is taking their, perhaps, first big risk with their 'baby' (the business they have nurtured so far) and they are taking that risk with people who hold all the power. Why should they trust us? Of course they are anxious, even if they don't show it, and it is our job to minimise that fear, and we do that by being completely truthful.

For many people in business a prospect is an opportunity to grab a new customer and make more money. For us it is an opportunity to build a relationship whether or not the prospect becomes a tenant. By not being attached to grabbing the customer, we free ourselves up to be totally honest about the building they are interested in, the good points and the worrying points about the lease (there are no worrying points with ours, but the prospects do not know that yet). Furthermore, lack of attachment to whether a prospective tenant moves in makes us independent of those customers who think that we need their custom. The ego of some people is palpable as they try to assert what little power they think they have as a prospective customer. Having said that, of course we are keen to acquire new tenants, and we are particularly enthusiastic in our approach to people that we feel understand us, for they are the ones we can build a strong relationship with.

Working examples of Openness and Honesty

1 **Encouraging comparisons.** Since most people choose premises based on location and price, we ask why they have come to us and whether they have looked at other sites near us. It is important they are able to make comparisons. This action builds the relationship through honesty. If they still choose to move in with us then they do so in the comfort of knowing that we are the best option for them – and we know that too.

2 **Growth opportunities.** We chat to them about their business and discuss possible growth in the future. We know that can happen and want them to understand how easily we can accommodate their growth. This action builds the relationship by showing that we care about their future requirements.

3 **Simple contracts.** We keep our contracts simple. Leases are only four pages long, and licence terms are on only one page. They are written in plain English, and we are happy to explain every clause so that the prospective tenant clearly understands their obligations to us as well as our obligations to them, and all without the need for a solicitor. This form of openness is a revelation for most prospective tenants, especially if they have had previous experience with leases, landlords, agents and solicitors.

4 **Assess Values.** Since our work is about building relationships, the show-round is an opportunity for the team member to ascertain whether the prospect holds similar Values to us and is someone they can build a relationship with. We are effectively interviewing them! And the team member makes this decision, not the managers or directors. I have been delighted with how our various team members have made these decisions, and interested in how techniques differ, but to the same end result.

We never abuse our power

On one occasion a prospective tenant started off a telephone conversation by insisting he would not pay our legal fees (in the days we used a solicitor for our leases). I simply asked why not. It transpired that he had been charged £1,500 by the landlord's solicitor for fees relating to negotiating a lease that did not go ahead. This made him fearful that it may happen again. Needless to say, I explained how we operate, and his attitude instantly changed. He relaxed. These seemingly little things have a big impact on how a landlord and tenant will work together. It is important to remember that in most cases the landlord has all the power, and it is our job to make the tenant realise that we will never abuse it.

Life is too short to be working with customers we cannot get on with.

5   **Look at both sides:** We explain all of the positives about being part of the community of the Park, and also the negatives (such as the poor bus service – meaning it is hard to recruit those without a car). It is better to make prospects aware of the negatives and allow them to decide to walk away than that they find out later and feel they have been duped. This kind of openness is refreshing to the prospective tenant, and attractive as well.

6   **Meet other tenants:** If they are still worried about how we may behave as landlords, we invite them to select a unit and we introduce them to the business owner of that unit for a private conversation about us. To be fair, I don't think anyone has taken us up on the offer yet.

Building a trusting relationship

While the Value of Openness and Honesty is pinned by us to the particular circumstances of prospective tenants, it is important to recognise its relevance to all things. It is a staple of the way we expect our team members to behave to all other people, including each other. When we behave with honesty, we lead the way for others to be honest with us – we cannot demand it, but we can notice it. Every act of honesty, especially when it comes from humility, is an act of building trusting relationships, and dishonesty damages the relationship. Every opportunity to be open, for example by being willing to answer all questions, should be considered an opportunity to build a relationship, while the opposite can close down a relationship.

Openness and Honesty are critical in any relationship, and therefore critical in business – or at least in the way we do business. There is no room in our business for dishonesty.

VALUE 2: Accommodating – for the sake of making people feel at home

We are so used to straplines being meaningless, just another marketing tool designed purely to sell product. We were worried that ours may be thought of in the same light, and we did not want ours to be inauthentic. We truly wanted to create a working environment where all our tenants and their staff could feel 'at home' when at work. We wanted the strapline to come to life; for it to be real.

One of the keys to making someone feel at home is to make them feel comfortable and that you understand them, and are happy to accommodate their needs, within reason. This is what happens when someone is invited into your home. You don't want your visitor at home to be scared of you, you don't wish to exert power over them. Rather you would consider the visitor an equal, someone you are proud to serve because you are honoured that they have come to visit. And so it can be on a business park if we so choose.

Business owners have enough problems running their business without us adding further to their anxiety by resisting the things they need, without good reason. The more we accommodate their property needs, the more they can relax with us and the more they can focus on their other business issues, which in turn means they are more likely to be successful, pay the rent and stay with us. It is common sense, and yet most commercial property owners do not behave in this way – to such an extent that what we do through common sense stands out as being unusual.

Working examples of being Accommodating

1   **A tenant needs some temporary additional space.** One tenant had a big and important contract to supply office furniture. Their production unit was quite small and they needed to deliver in large loads, so they needed to store finished items until there was sufficient product to fill the delivery truck. We had an empty unit

and made it available to them, at no cost. We accommodated their short-term needs. We could have charged full rent, and that would be seen to be reasonable by many. Instead we chose to understand their need and not take advantage. This builds the relationship at no real cost to us – the unit was empty anyway. In the long term, and with consistency in our approach, this generosity is remembered by the tenant and is factored into growth decisions and conversations. In other words, they are more likely to stay with us as they grow, and more likely to say positive things about us to others.

2 **A local charity needs temporary space.** Similar to the example above, at the suggestion of our housekeeper who knew the charity, we allowed them to use a large, empty unit without charge for a few months to box up parcels for Christmas to send to disadvantaged children abroad. Some of our team volunteered to help as well. There was no real cost to us, we were just doing a favour. The charity were so grateful they issued various press releases and we ended up with a lot of publicity.

3 **A tenant gets into financial difficulty.** He phones to explain that he will not be able to pay the rent for three months. What we do is to try to understand what has happened. The first important point is to recognise the tenant's honesty in coming forward, and the courage that takes. We will go and see the tenant, talk over a coffee, listen to his story and what he proposes to do about it. Normally then we would accommodate his needs by, for example, allowing the rent-free period, and request the back rent be added to future rents. No contracts, no fear, just trust. We recognise that our true investment is in the tenant, not in the building. In doing this, we build the relationship fully aware of the risk that the tenant may not make it, but knowing that he is aware that we are rooting for him.

4 **Security.** After a few break-ins, we recognised the need to add security to the Park. The question was how to do that without

No pressure

In a more standard scenario the landlord is usually represented by an agent, whose job is to collect the rent. If rent has not been collected, the agent has to explain to the landlord. The agent at the very least will give the tenant a hard time and exert immense pressure. The agent has little empathy for the tenant's problems, and no incentive to accommodate their needs.

Incidentally if the tenant goes bankrupt we would stand to lose three months rent – perhaps more – but our loss is minor compared to the tenant's loss of a business, and at least we have done a bit to help. If the tenant succeeds, we have retained a fan and we feel good about what we have done, which builds team spirit.

And finally on this example, it is amazing how often that when one tenant leaves, another tenant arrives, often prepared to pay more rent, often with a better attitude and a better business model. In my view we never lose in the long run by being accommodating.

impacting too much on the tenants' businesses. In some parks, the security is onerous and expensive, and the tenants pay for it as a service charge. We chose to upgrade the hawthorn hedging, which forms an excellent prickly boundary to the Park, by adding thick mesh fencing, which is both impregnable and well hidden. We also chose to add automatic barriers at the entrance which are raised during working hours, and opened at night and weekends by a regularly changing barrier code. These simple and relatively inexpensive methods take effort to work out. We do not copy anyone else, but rather formulate a solution that puts the tenants' needs first. And we still do not impose a service charge.

A two-way process

By practising being accommodating, and discussing it as a team, it becomes normal behaviour. We trust the team, which frees all members to be accommodating to our tenants, as long as they then explain what they have done. All team members are given authority, are expected to behave responsibly, and are expected to be accountable for their actions – and by that I mean they have to be honest about their mistakes not that they have any losses deducted from their salaries! Often decisions around being accommodating are discussed as a team before going ahead. The team are more likely to be accommodating to tenants they trust will not abuse our good nature.

When tenants see us being accommodating this is just one way where they start to trust us and appreciate us as fellow human beings, as equals. They start to feel 'at home'. Our team make our strapline come to life.

Being accommodating must not always be a one-way process. As with all the Values, it is a two-way process. We cannot insist, but we hope that while we are accommodating to our tenants so they respond with respect for us and what we are trying to achieve by making the Park feel like home.

We also hope that by following our example they will be accommodating to others on the Park. Some tenants share equipment such as fork-lift trucks, or take in parcels for neighbours. This builds community, creates friendships and generally makes life easier for everyone. We do what we can to encourage collaboration by introducing tenants to each other, recommending tenants who can supply others, and talking to new tenants about what existing tenants do. We produce a directory of businesses and a quarterly newsletter. All of these things help to build a thriving business community, which is fundamentally different from simply managing a disparate set of buildings with people working in them.

VALUE 3: Commitment – for the sake of delivering a service which exceeds expectation

At work, we are expected to be committed and we tend to think that what is required is a commitment to the company in order to help make more money for the company. The employee's reward is a salary and the prospect of a career. Commitment has come to mean working hard for, and being loyal to, the company which provides you with employment. Commitment has become a subconscious contract, consideration for which is in the form of prospective career advancement and financial return.

That is not what we mean. For us commitment is about how we behave towards others, and particularly to our tenants (customers). We commit to deliver a service which is better than that which a tenant would normally expect of a landlord.

Service is not the same as being 'in servitude'. Servitude is akin to slavery, doing what you are told to do, or what is expected of you. Service is something we do willingly. In fact, service is the higher calling which we can all aspire to.

The most fulfilling things we do in life are when we help, or care for, others. To focus only on ever-higher earnings is self-serving, and is not fulfilling. And that is true of both an individual, and of a business.

For us, service is about caring for the needs of our tenants. Service alone is not good enough; that is only what our tenants expect and pay for. Caring with empathy, and understanding of their current and future needs, is beyond expectation. It is what Tony Hsieh, CEO of Zappos – who wrote the story of his company in Delivering Happiness – would call the 'Wow! Factor', and it is what Vernon Hill of Metro

Bank calls having 'fans, not customers'. This is what we aspire to. It is one factor which elevates us above our competitors.

Working examples of Commitment

1 **Rapid response.** Every person on the team is able to make a decision to help a tenant without normally referring to a manager or colleague. This speeds up decisions and makes the tenant feel valued. If the decision could have been better, then the team will discuss and learn, but rarely change it, for that would undermine the very authority we are trying to allow them. Recently a friend who rents premises on another business park explained how it took three weeks for the landlord to change a light bulb. The actual impact of that poor service was not that the tenant was waiting, but that it showed quite clearly that he was not being cared for, and that the landlord is not interested in the relationship. Of course, this also has a marketing impact as the tenant will tell others about the poor service.

2 **Contractors.** We are careful to use contractors in or around the tenants' premises who respect our tenants and their staff. The work of contractors is an extension of our service and we expect them to have similar Values. A 'service beyond expectation' extends to how they behave towards our tenants. On a major building project the contractor, on understanding our ethos, decided, without prompting by us, to add a weekly report to his service. For the whole contract period of nine months these weekly reports were distributed to our tenants so that they were aware in advance of any potentially disruptive work.

3 **Caring for tenants.** We notice when tenants need more or less space. We can then be aware when space becomes available such that when tenants ask we can give an immediate response. In serving our tenants, we are constantly considering what we perceive as their needs even before they do so themselves. There

is an art to juggling space requirements with space availability which involves looking to the near future and caring for tenants needs. This is one area in which we excel.

Relationships in practice

In the world of commercial property, it is common that once the lease is signed there is no need for communication between landlord and tenant. The relationship is defined by the lease contract. There is no need for further service, no need to care. Where in the contract does it say that a light bulb has to be changed in less than three weeks? The contractual obligation becomes the template for behaviour, or the excuse for poor behaviour.

For our team, everything stems from building a good relationship with our tenants. The lease is merely a formality which defines behavioural boundaries (the tenant is required only to pay the rent, keep the place tidy, and not cause a nuisance to their neighbours). If we have to refer to the lease, then something is wrong with the relationship.

Doing the right thing

In a sense, poor behaviour is a microcosm of what is wrong in our society. The reliance on contractual obligation rather than doing the right thing allows the excuse that there is nothing wrong with behaviour that most can see as self-serving. Immoral behaviour seems these days to be excusable if it is not illegal. Rules are not broken, but our society is.

Our commitment to providing the best possible service can only happen when we build relationships with our customers. Without that, service is not necessary.

We cannot *expect* our tenants to have a commitment to us, in other words there is no reciprocation as there can be with other Values, but I have noticed that by behaving this way, our tenants tend to stay. Perhaps the negative of that comment is better – that we are not giving them any reason to leave. I do hope that by our example to them, our tenants can commit to a service beyond expectation to their customers – and I am sure that many do.

This is the 'pay it forward' concept which is how our Values-based approach is spreading.

A key element of commitment is the recognition that creativity and innovation can and should come from any member of the team. When the desire is to provide a service beyond expectation then anything is possible; any new idea can be embraced. Any member of the team who holds this Value (and we expect them all to) can also assume the authority to make changes to improve our service, as long as they also accept responsibility for their actions. We aspire to be the best that we can possibly be, with no limits.

Another key element of this particular Value is that it represents the importance of making change happen. The strapline makes it clear that the service 'exceeds expectation'. If there is no improvement then the service will tend to be 'at expectation'. Continual improvement is both possible and necessary to keep ahead of the competition and every member of the team plays their part.

However, in service there must also be balance. Some tenants, when we provide exceptional service, just expect more. This is especially true of those who have not experienced working with other landlords. Sometimes we have to courteously decline a tenant's request for the sake of balance and fairness to all tenants.

The desire to give better service is not the same as responding to an expectation. One comes from grace, the other comes from control.

VALUE 4: Fairness – for the sake of establishing loyalty and trust

Fairness means different things to different people and it is important to ensure, when you are building relationships, that both parties believe that the outcome of any transaction is fair. It is not enough that you feel you are being fair to someone, if they don't think you are being fair to them. You need to understand the other person's perspective before being able to judge what is fair. It is a two-way process.

For example, when negotiating a rent review one method is to have in mind a higher rent, knowing that the tenant will try to negotiate you down. At the same time you expect the tenant to start with a low rent, knowing that you will try to negotiate him up. This process turns the negotiation into a competition, where both parties are trying to win. While this form of negotiation will result in an outcome which will seem to be fair, in fact both parties will be less than satisfied, and the process does nothing towards building loyalty and trust. I call this competitive fairness.

We have an alternative. Our rent reviews are friendly chats. Each team member is building a relationship with the tenant, and each will work out the best way of doing this; for one it may be taking an interest in the tenant's team members, for another it may be more related to the business, the industry they are in, and prospects for the future. The point is that we are building relationships; building trust. By the time we start to talk about the rent review, mutual trust has already emerged, anxiety has diminished, and the tenant is prepared to accept a reasonable review as long as we are able to explain why we believe it to be fair, and as long as we listen to their points too. I call this empathetic fairness.

Empathetic fairness is, or should be, normal, while competitive fairness is a mask for being self-serving. If your prime focus is to make money, especially in the short term, then if a negotiation is fair it is by accident rather than by design – fairness does not come into the equation.

It follows that the Value of Fairness as a single word is pointless because it means different things to different people, and such a Value would be divisive. Our strapline of loyalty and trust therefore is essential to make it clear to the team the purpose of fairness.

Negotiations in order to get your way, even if you think they are fair, do not build loyalty and trust; understanding the other person's perspective does.

When people feel they have been fairly treated, especially by someone who could have power or control over them, then they begin to trust – or the trust they have deepens, and they tend to become loyal – or their loyalty strengthens.

Conversely if someone does something unfair to you and you can do nothing about it, then there is a tendency to internalise it and it festers. You can feel powerless and uncomfortable. Would you be loyal to that person again? Would you trust them?

Loyalty is a prize that is earned, not demanded or bought. People grant you their loyalty, and they can take it away. By treating people with respect, and by being consistently fair, you will be doing your best to maintain and build the relationship. And incidentally this is not price sensitive. Low prices do not encourage loyalty. We are more likely to be loyal to people we trust will serve us well, and who charge a fair price.

When a tenant vacates, that does not mean he or she is disloyal, merely that an appropriate business decision has not been in our favour. A tenant can remain loyal even when ceasing to buy from us. Many of our past tenants still recommend us.

VALUE 5: Courtesy – for the sake of creating an environment where people feel valued

Courtesy is not just about opening the door for someone – though we do that! Courtesy is about care and consideration for another, showing a little kindness for no other reason than we want to. It makes us feel good, too, so why would anyone choose to be discourteous?

Business, however, seems to be the exception, where it is easy to excuse poor behaviour as 'it's just business', even though in reality 'it's just poor behaviour'. Whenever anyone excuses themselves by saying 'it's just business', what they are doing is masking their discourtesy and trying to tell themselves that what they did was acceptable. It isn't.

Exerting your control over another, abusing people with your power, making money out of another person's misery or out of devastation to the environment – these things all happen in the name of 'business'. Well it is not the kind of business we want to have anything to do with.

In our company, we do not tolerate poor behaviour. We choose not to work with people who show that they are discourteous to us or to others. Bad behaviour from our customers can reflect badly on us, and we have been known not to renew a lease for tenants who consistently treat others discourteously.

Working examples of Discourtesy

1   **Be polite or leave.** In the story of his New York restaurant business, Setting the Table, Danny Meyer explains how he publicly kicked out of his restaurant a wealthy customer who was abusive to one of his waitresses. Quite right! I would do the same. Discourtesy, especially when it comes with the arrogance of someone with

money, or position, who thinks that gives them permission to behave like that, is an abomination. Business leaders need to be more prominent in their disdain of such behaviour, for in doing what Danny did, favouring his staff over his desire to make profit, we set the tone for how we expect our team to behave, and what is acceptable for them to tolerate.

2 **Standing up to Discourtesy.** In a similar episode on the Park, we once had a visitor who regularly used our meeting rooms. On one occasion she was particularly and unnecessarily abusive to our receptionist, Amie. When Amie was brave enough to report this episode at the next team meeting I made it clear that if it happened again she had my permission to tell the customer to 'F*** off'. The bluntness was deliberate so that all the team would know how I felt. That kind of discourtesy has no place at Jennings. Amie later reported that she and the customer now get on 'like a house on fire'. I had subconsciously given Amie permission to stand up to the customer, and her change in attitude was sufficient to bring the customer into line as an equal.

Courtesy is King – the gift of equality

I was taught as an accountant that 'cash is king'. And then in business I learned that was wrong, and that 'the customer is king'. Well I now know that is also wrong. The truth is that 'courtesy is king'. Courtesy helps to build relationships, and relationships build businesses.

I have noticed that by extending courtesy to others we give them permission to respond in kind. People seem to reflect back our behaviours to them.

Courtesy is a gift that is within the power of every person to withhold or to give generously. Courtesy is a Value which we can all hold and give out equally, and so is another Value that oozes equality.

Sad state of affairs

It seems that in the field of commercial letting there is little room for courtesy. Buildings are the assets which must be protected at all costs against potentially erroneous tenants. Leases are set up by the landlord to control the tenant. The landlord's agents and solicitors work for the sole benefit of their client and have no interest in courtesy as their job is to protect their client against the possibility of the tenant taking advantage. What a shame that this has become a norm in the industry. No wonder prospective tenants often arrive at our doors with fears and anxieties.

At Jennings we extend courtesy at every opportunity. This is not done to impress, nor to make sales. This is done naturally, and it has the effect of making people feel valued because, quite simply, they are. Furthermore when we are courteous, and especially when it is appreciated, it makes us feel good about ourselves and strengthens the team's resolve to do it more.

VALUE 6: Trust – for the sake of enabling relationships to grow

Trust is the one Value that pulls them all together. All of the previous five Values help to build trust, and trust is imperative to building lasting relationships, and lasting relationships are a fundamental base for good business.

So let's break that down.

Real business, and especially business done by the vast majority – the owner-managed businesses – is mainly predicated on building relationships with others – your team, your customers and your providers. As they say at Metro Bank 'Fans, not customers'. Fans who will spread the word about how amazing you are – amazing product, service, after sales – anything which makes you stand out from the crowd. Fans bring in new customers and in my experience almost all small businesses grow primarily through recommendation.

Your fans need to trust that you are not going to abuse them, that you are not going to put your own profit before their needs, that you are not self-serving. In business we are providers of something that another person needs. That does not give us a right to abuse that position, rather it gives us a responsibility to do our best for those who are attracted to our door.

One has to wonder if even that is enough. Being treated well as a customer is one thing. Understanding that you are being treated that way because they value you as a person, rather than just as a customer, is another thing altogether. Perhaps Metro Bank is one part of a journey towards better banking. Perhaps we are delighted as customers to be treated as fans, but do we really believe that they are treating us this way for any other reason than to build their own profits – albeit in a nice way? Consider the new 'challenger banks', such as Tandem, which is starting its banking operations by asking the customers what they want. The CEO is visible on social media, we know something about him. He seems trustworthy, and perhaps we are more likely to use his bank for that reason alone. Perhaps an even better example is Guy Watson, owner of Riverford Organic Farmers (www.riverford.co.uk). He writes a regular blog that goes out to all his customers in which he explains his view on chemical-free farming. Trust is more than being a fan, it is also about understanding intent.

As with loyalty, we cannot demand that another person trusts us. We have to earn it. The only way to do that is to extend our trust first.

We have to show that we are trustworthy, which is not always easy. People who have had their trust abused in the past are more likely to be more cautious in the future, as it is a natural response to put in place barriers to stop us being hurt again. Those defensive barriers limit the ability to develop relationships and it will take longer to earn their trust.

As business owners we need to not only be comfortable extending trust to others, but also be able to encourage all of our team to extend trust as well. For some it is difficult to extend trust because of the fear that our trust will be rejected, or that others will just take advantage. The truth is that the vast majority of people do not abuse our trust, they respond in kind because they appreciate you showing trust in them, and then a relationship can begin.

When someone does abuse our trust – then we face a choice:

1   We can retaliate. Often this is done under the mask of following orders, or responding according to the contract, or just out of spite. Retaliation just brings us down to their level. Retaliation is part of the race to the bottom. We can be so much better than that.

2   We can assume that there is a fault in our administration process that allows someone to abuse our trust. The simple way to remedy

that fault is to set up controls so that the abuse can never happen again. This is a common source of rules and regulations which plague small businesses. Rules effectively demonstrate that we do not trust anyone. Furthermore they rarely prevent the abuser from trying again – the problem lies with the attitude, not the action.

3   We can accept that this is a person with whom we cannot build a relationship, and let them go, in other words we would cease to work with them.

Our choice at Jennings is the third in that list. No hassle, no drama, but we do need to quickly identify those who do not share our Values, or do not respect us for what we have done for them, recognising the need to understand the difference between those who find it hard to return our trust in them, and those who abuse it. How we do that is explained fully in the next chapter.

In real life, of course, we don't suddenly decide someone is untrustworthy. These feelings grow upon us. A series of events occur that lead us to believe that a person cannot be trusted. Perhaps it could be someone who continually says they will do something, and then does not do it. Perhaps it is someone who regularly ignores the rules in their own self-interest. Perhaps it is someone whose actions are continuously self-serving. Even then, we still try to understand first, then confront them with their behaviour, and finally, if the behaviour continues, the relationship will diminish.

When you have established trust, then things work faster. It is perhaps worth reading Stephen Covey's book, *The Speed of Trust*, for a more in-depth understanding on this subject, and with lots of real-life examples. From a Jennings perspective, because our tenants trust us, they are not suspicious of anything we do. Their assumption is that what we are doing is in their interest, taking their needs into account, and done in the best way we can. They understand our intent because they trust us.

Working examples of Trust

1 **Resurfacing a road.** Out of Courtesy, we would let the tenants know the details of the forthcoming work. They rarely question it, let alone complain, because they trust us. They know that we will have taken their needs into account and will do it in the best way possible. This may seem like a minor point, but it strikes at the heart of the business. If there is a poor relationship, or one based on the landlord being 'in control', then the tenants may feel that their needs have not been considered and this will increase the bad feeling, damage what little relationship there is, and lead the tenant to bad-mouth the landlord – and that impacts on the landlords marketing ability, leading to empty properties. If there is a good relationship, then even if the tenant does feel aggrieved, they will have no problems in asking what is happening and what we have done to limit the effect on their business. We get the chance to explain ourselves and adapt to help them. This builds the relationship and adds to our marketing prospects.

2 **Reducing rent.** Sometimes tenants go through difficult periods in their business. On one occasion a tenant explained that everyone was mucking in, and that the staff had all agreed to a 9% pay cut. We immediately agreed to match that with a 9% cut in rent, trusting that when the staff got a subsequent pay-rise, then so would we. There was no need for a contract to bind this agreement, which was concluded with a handshake. It sounds old-fashioned, but be in no doubt that this helped cement a very good working relationship not only with the owner, but also the team, who recognised that we would 'stand with them'.

Mutual trust is a cornerstone of good business, and that is why it is one of our Values.

CHAPTER EIGHT

The Impact of Values

Demonstrating how we live
our Values

Integrity is choosing courage over comfort; choosing what is right over what is fun, fast, or easy; and choosing to practice our values rather than simply professing them.

Brené Brown – American scholar
and author

What we had achieved was to set in stone, with clarity, a set of behavioural parameters (not rules), for the team to follow. These Values were an expression of how we were behaving, and we believed they could be put forward as a platform for the whole team so that we would be working from the same base.

We had no idea whether six was the right number of Values, or whether there were more that we did not have time to uncover, but perhaps could be added later. We did know that each Value would have meaning well beyond what we had set down on paper. We felt that the Values would have impact, but we did not know in what way.

This chapter explains some of the ways the Values have impacted on the business.

Disruption

Having set our Values, the next job was to communicate them to the team. We needed the team to understand what would be expected of them in the future. Our coach volunteered to run a team event for half a day, while I manned the reception. The Values were less than enthusiastically received by the team; some liked them, some did not. Over the next six months half of the team found jobs elsewhere. To be clear, we did not make them redundant, rather they chose to leave. And I cannot say that they left because of the Values, but the coincidence of timing makes this seem likely. Perhaps there was something about the Values that did not sit right with them. Setting Values, on the face of it, was quite destructive, and very unsettling for the team.

I won't pretend that this process was easy. There was no one whose example we could copy, no one who could identify with what we were trying to do. It was unnerving, but I did not waver in my belief that we were heading in the right direction. Certainly we could not go back.

With hindsight, I now realise that those who did not naturally accept the Values as a basis for our collective way of working were the ones who left. Sometimes it is important to dismantle before you can build up again on a solid foundation. While it was initially uncomfortable, it did present us with the opportunity to recruit a new team.

Recruitment

We started recruiting people who shared our Values. We did not have a template for doing this. I am not convinced that a formal framework, even if based on our Values, would have worked. Instead we chose people we liked, who seemed to be interested in our business and who had personality. We took on one receptionist because she added as an afterthought at the foot of her CV: 'And I bake a mean cake!' We like cake. The point of interest here is not that she can cook, but that she had the guts to add something a bit unusual to her formal CV. It showed personality and a willingness to do something different without worrying about how other people would react. At one point we interviewed two people for the role of personal assistant. We liked them both, so created an additional job and recruited both of them. During the interview process it is natural, in my view, to be attracted to people who hold similar Values to yourself.

We took to asking our existing receptionists their opinion of the job applicants, as all applicants first arrived at the office before their interview. Were they courteous, open and honest? Did they treat the receptionists as equals? We also started to include other members of staff in the interview process. We were, after all, recruiting into the team so it was important to allow the team to be involved in the process. Also we felt that including junior staff in the interview would form part of their training.

To an extent it takes some courage not to simply employ the person with the most experience. That seems the obvious thing to do, the route that will be accompanied by the least blame if something goes wrong. It helped in our case that I did not consider experience in the property industry to be useful for us. Consider, for example, a choice of a bookkeeper being someone who has experience but is a bit miserable and set in their ways, or someone with little or no experience but bags of enthusiasm, willing to learn. The first person would do the job competently but at the risk of upsetting the team, and the second would fit in with the team, but at the risk of not being able to do the job. In my view it is easier to train someone to perform a job than to train someone to fit in with an established team.

This is the point at which we defined our decision to recruit for 'attitude above aptitude'. If someone has the right attitude, then they will be willing to learn. If someone comes with relevant experience, they may not fit into the team ethos and they could bring a qualifications-based ego into the team which would inevitably be disruptive.

To build a team of people who are happy working together, attitude and behaviour are crucial, and for us we use our Values as a means of establishing whether an applicant will fit into the team. In other words we select people only if they share our Values.

And just finally on recruitment. I was interested in the Zappos method of recruitment. They have a six-week induction programme at the end of which they offer $2,000 to each applicant not to take the job. The idea is to root out those who are only doing it for the money. Where the business considers profit to be an outcome rather than a prime objective, then you want your people to consider their salary to be an outcome, not an objective.

Law of attraction

Some years after we set out our Values, I held a team meeting where I had asked each member of the team to name a tenant they particularly liked and why. It was a lovely, uplifting meeting as they each named two tenants (they found it too difficult to narrow their choice to one), and they said some positive things about the people they put forward. We concluded that the people we like 'are friendly, have a sense of humour, have a personal touch, are interested in us, join in with our events, say nice things about us, and are humble despite their success'. We explored that further and agreed that the common attributes of the people we like are that they are: courteous, honourable, appreciative, hard-working, trust us, are honest, cheerful, fair and considerate. It is not really a surprise that those qualities reflect our Values.

A few months later, I ran a similar exercise with the team except that they had to name the tenant that they least liked, and why. The conclusion to this exercise was that the attributes we do not like are when people are: unreasonable, dishonest, manipulative, untrusting, unappreciative, demanding, rude, arrogant and unfair. Basically people who are not aligned to our Values.

What was interesting was that all of the team found the second exercise much harder, and many of the suggested names were tenants who had recently left the Park. I was curious and on checking found that almost all of them, one way or another, did not fit in with our Values.

For me, this is a clear example of the law of attraction at work. Like-minded people are attracted to each other. If we honestly and consistently communicate our Values, we not only attract people who behave in the same way, but also positively push away those who do not. If that is so, and I truly believe it is, then the more we focus on our Values, the better for the business. We are building a 'tribe' (see Seth Godin's book *Tribes*) of people around us who we can trust, and who serve us well. That tribe is made up of team members, customers, suppliers, contractors and professionals. I have no doubt that this process has contributed to the success of the business.

Looking back, I have realised that this is a continually evolving process. We are getting better at expressing our Values, for example in the wording on our website and on our social media sites. This has resulted in a far better quality of customer being attracted to our door, and I think it has pushed out those who do not share our Values. Prospective tenants now are almost exclusively people we want to do business with, and that filtering process makes our working life so much easier.

Communicating Values

We wanted to ensure that our Values really became an intrinsic part of our company and we set about ensuring that they permeated every aspect of our work, internal and external.

Implementing the Values internally

It did not take much encouragement for our team to start chatting about the Values. Initially this came about as they started comparing how they behaved in relation to the Values, mainly in a humorous way: 'that wasn't very courteous' – when someone had made coffee for themselves, but not asked anyone else; ' where is your commitment'– when someone had to leave the office early. I guess humour is a good way to start when you are a bit uncertain about something new. Later the team started commenting on the behaviour of others outside the team. They began to notice behaviour which was not in line with our Values, initially with customers (See 'When Values are abused' below).

We hold weekly team meetings where we discuss our various contacts with tenants, so that we all know what is going on. The team meetings throw up alerts which help us to build relationships. For example, if a tenant has a medical issue or a family problem then one of the team may feel moved to go and have a chat. At these meetings, I was able to highlight behaviour of team members that was in line with our Values, giving praise and showing appreciation. I was also able to comment when it was against our Values, never criticising but just bringing it to notice so as not to induce fear of failure around our Values. I wanted all of the team to use these meetings as a way of growing and sharing best practice in line with our Values. We cannot all get it all right all the time, but if most of us get it mainly right most of the time, then we have a basis for continual improvement. Sometimes I would have a quiet word in private if something had gone a bit wrong.

The point is that slowly the team started changing behaviour, and at the same time they relaxed into the idea that they could do their jobs without stress, just by simply being themselves. They had, after all, been recruited based on their Values. It is unnatural and creates dis-ease – such as stress, strokes, heart problems and depression – when people at work are expected do things that are against their Values in the name of maximising short-term profit. It is unnatural because it goes against our basic human desires to care about each other.

Over time it became easier to do, even natural. Furthermore I noticed that team members started emulating me, and so now the team members are constantly monitoring each other (in a good way), shaping the way the Values are expressed. This is now happening without my input, and it is a joy to watch it evolve in this way.

Implementing the Values externally

We decided that we needed a new brand that better reflected our Values and we wanted something totally different. The website and all other marketing material (newsletter, diaries, mugs, pens and so on) give us an opportunity to communicate to others how we choose to behave and we wanted it to be really meaningful.

We chose a branding agency that could grasp what we were trying to achieve. Once they understood us, it was great to work with them. They were excited about our objective – to reflect through the brand that we really do put our Values ahead of the drive towards ever-increasing profit.

They reviewed our competitors and noticed that almost all other commercial property companies used cold colours as a central part of their brand – mainly blues. The type of words competitors used on their websites and general marketing were also cold, reflecting a 'professional' service – one that put profit and control at the forefront. People in business tend to think that being 'professional' is a good thing, but it is not, especially once you understand that business is primarily about building relationships.

We wanted to get our message across with subtlety. If we rammed it home that, for example 'we develop best-in-class relationships', then no one would believe us – it would just be another corporate sound-bite to those who don't know us. Our website had to get the message across with subtlety that through our Values we really do create a 'home for your business'; a safe and comfortable environment. Authentic relationships which reflect equality, independence and balance are an outcome of our Values.

Adding Values

For a few years I wondered if we should add some more Values to our list. Would this help? I asked the team if they had any ideas. Two came up: Fun and Kindness.

Fun is a great Value to have in a business. We get so wound up with the belief that it is just 'a job' or a means to earn a living. Why should it not also be fun? In my experience, business owners really enjoy what they do. Yes, running a business has its stresses and anxieties, but alongside that is the excitement of the ride, and behind all that is a sense of achievement, freedom and fun. And if it is fun for the owner, why cannot it be fun for the rest of the team? Humour cuts through obstinacy. Fun undermines the stress created by the profit motive. Fun is a good Value.

Kindness is another great Value. Being kind to someone is not so much a gift to the person you are being kind to, but a gift to yourself. It is uplifting whether or not the other person or anyone else notices your kind act.

I considered these and other potential new Values. Fun I think is an outcome for us anyway. It was not necessary to specify that we want the team to have fun, it has been a natural process when the team members realise that they are able to be themselves at work. They relax, they are at ease, and humour naturally emits from everyone. Similarly kindness is a natural product of ease. When there is no reason to be unkind, people are kind. Pretty obvious. Our Values of Courtesy and Accommodating come from a sense of kindness to others. I did not feel it appropriate to add an extra Value when kindness was emanating from our existing Values.

I came to the conclusion that the six Values are very clear and focused. Adding to them would throw them into uncertainty. I want the team to consider them set in stone, not adaptable. If one could be added then another could be added, or one could be removed. Best to keep it simple, concise and regular.

Our Values are our Values. They are not up for negotiation.

The wider application of Values

Much of what we have considered above is with Values in relation to dealing with customers, but it is important to recognise that Values form the core for establishing good and trusting relationships with everyone.

Providers

So we apply our Values to our providers. We extend trust to them, we are fair in agreeing a price for their work, we pay promptly, we express our gratitude for the service they provide. We want to build a relationship of trust just as we do with our customers. At the same time we notice, and have expectations of, their behaviour towards us. There is more on how we do this in the sections below on Assessment and Challenging.

Where we can, we work with local providers who share our Values. When we request a provider to perform a task – whether they are professionals, contractors or suppliers – we know that it will be done to the best of their ability (Commitment). We do not have to check their work, or their price, or waste time with competitive quotes because we trust them to be fair. This way of working demands that a trusting relationship is at the core of the transaction. This is the antithesis of most business-like thinking where fear of being taken advantage of leads to requests for quotes and then selecting the provider who offers the cheapest price.

The problem with the cheapest-price culture is that it takes a lot of time and effort. Time getting several quotes to select the cheapest, more time spent making sure the supplier turns up when they said they would, and effort expended making sure they do the job well. Where there is no trust, then micro-management has to be the style of operating, and it is stressful to all concerned. This fear-based approach is often angled in such a way that the buyer cannot be blamed if something goes wrong. Not only is this a waste of time, but also this process makes it likely the provider will only do as they are told. In contrast we expect the provider to feel free to suggest better ways forward, using their knowledge and experience to our benefit (a service beyond expectation). In this way, our providers becomes equals, contributors and part of our team.

Occasionally providers take advantage of our good nature. If necessary, we call them out (challenge them), and in the worst cases, pay them off. We would not work with them again. Our Values allow us to identify poor behaviour as well as people with integrity, and the benefit to us is that working only with people we trust is easier, and in the long run more efficient. Yes, there is a possibility of failure if you trust someone, and yes the price may be higher than you could get elsewhere, but the advantages hugely outweigh the potential disadvantages.

Professionals

Professionals are a special case. Many operate bounded by the rules and regulations of their profession, whereas we want to work with professionals who understand our needs. Many come from a position of 'the customer needs our expertise' (arrogance or ego) whereas we want to work with those who recognise that they are an equal part of our team. Many are closed-minded, thinking only of their own part of the whole, whereas we want to work with those who see the big picture and are able to adapt for the sake of the project. We want to work with professionals whose Values are similar to ours and we are quite prepared to pay more for the privilege of working with these precious people. Our Values allow us to identify professionals with whom we do not want to work, as well as those who we do want to build a relationship with.

Corporate providers

It is important to be especially careful when working with corporate providers. Banks can be very difficult, as many small business owners will attest. While a single bank manager may share our Values, they are powerless to prevent directives from above. This is the problem with corporates – you build trust with a person, not a corporation. If the person we do trust has a decision undermined by a manager who we don't know, then there can be no trust. I have met many tenants and friends in business who have been brought to their knees by corporate antics. My advice is to be very wary when dealing with corporate customers or providers, and don't let them become too big a part of your business, because then they can control you. Control, or abuse of power, for the sake of maximising profits is in the nature of corporates.

Don't be bullied

I well remember one tenant whose main customer told him (and other suppliers) that he had to reduce his prices by 5% a year for the next few years. The tenant refused. Now this is a big thing. He risked losing a high proportion of his turnover. However, he reckoned they needed him more than he needed them. Eventually they acquiesced and he held his prices. In doing so he retained his independence – he would not be bullied by them.

The team

Having built a team based on the Values, we can expect that they will naturally implement those Values in how they behave towards each other, and it is important to notice it.

There is a team spirit revolving around shared behaviours which unites people.

We know that collectively our behaviours are defined by the 'for the sake ofs'.

- Our Commitment to each other is to provide a service to each other which is beyond expectation. There has to be an acceptance that all tasks make a whole, and that how we do a job may impact on another team member. Understanding the impacts of our work on other team members is very important in building a strong team.

- We are Fair with each other and that builds loyalty and trust within the team.

- We are Honest and Open with each other in order to minimise anxieties. There is no back-stabbing, or whispering behind backs or other corporate/bureaucratic nonsense in our team.

- We Accommodate each other's needs. Where one team member is struggling then others will help out, in the sure knowledge that the team would do the same for them.

- We Trust each other. Mutual trust is what binds us and makes our unity rock solid.

Equality and Competitiveness

When you are aiming to develop a group of people into a team, then you need to step back and think about equality and competitiveness.

Equality is uniting. Operating to our Values brings us back to equality and thus unity.

- Everyone has an equal ability to behave according to our Values, to do things which make each other feel at home, feel valued, feel trusted.

- Everyone has an equal opportunity to innovate, to try things out, to just get on and do something positive without fear of the consequences of failure.

- Everyone has an equal opportunity to try out new skills, to face and conquer their fears with the support and encouragement of other team members, and that helps to grow personal self-belief, which strengthens both the individual and the team.

This all happens when we trust each other in a team. When we feel free to give to each other in this way, then we do indeed receive in abundance. There is not a single person in the team who has not benefitted from this culture and grown in their self-confidence about who they are.

Inequality is divisive. Inequality is inevitable in a team when the focus is on things like what job you do, how much you get paid, how big your office is, how many people you manage.

When we compete with each other in a team; that is divisive. There can be only one winner. But if we challenge ourselves to improve (and thus compete with ourselves), we are all winners. The hierarchical system encourages competition within a team, but our Values give us all a platform for self-improvement that transcends competition.

By focussing on what unites us, a team can celebrate individual diversity.

On the other hand, if you recruit someone who is a taker, who believes that they need to compete to get promotion, or who is selfishly manipulative in any way, then that behaviour must be identified and eliminated. The quicker this happens the better. The Jennings team is good at recruiting people who share our Values, but we have got it wrong on occasion and probably will do again. Where we have got it wrong, the prospective team member does not pass our three-month probation period. However, it is possible to be kind and caring with rejection, and I believe those rejected have understood why, and gone on to find other jobs which suit them better.

Life and work are not separate

Balance between work and other aspects of life is often determined by how much time is spent on each. In my view it is much more important to view work/life balance in terms of behaviour. It is how accepting we are of one another that marks us as human beings, not how much time we spend with each other. Thus we can still be friends with someone we have not seen for many years.

The balance of life changes as we evolve, and in a culture where we evolve quickly through the continuous application of our Values, then it is inevitable that we take the new 'us' home to our families and friends. They notice the change as we evolve into who we really are.

In my view, the change in people is beautiful, and most family and friends would agree. However there are some who are frightened by change, and where those people are family or friends of team members, then that can impact on their personal relationships. In these circumstances team members can wobble.

We cannot, and must not, separate the worker from the person. People are human beings, not human resources. It is inevitable that sometimes life at home will have an emotional impact on a team member. What often happens in business is that the worker is expected to work as if emotions are irrelevant. People learn to hide their emotions. People learn to put on a mask as they come through the door to work. They pretend to be strong. They are not themselves. This behaviour goes against our Values.

At Jennings, problems are shared. We allow the space for team members to care about each other. Opening up at work to someone about what is happening in your home life is cathartic. Taking a moment to do this is hugely important, and yet often overlooked or ignored in business. Many people of course open up naturally with people they trust. We do it as a team; it is part of our service to each other.

Team meetings, for example, often start with a 'check-in' where each person says a little bit about what is happening for them or how they are feeling right now.

Sometimes problems at home can be so impactful that it affects the behaviour of the team member. They may do things that on the surface are against our Values. In these circumstances it is easy to criticise or blame, but we must look at the situation with empathy. Why is this happening, and how can we help? It is only through empathy and understanding that we can help our fellow team members get through any crisis.

There is also the issue of work/life balance that can be so contentious in an ordinary office. No one notices if you come in early but if you leave on time, you can be criticised. It then becomes 'normal' to work later and later. Inevitably that will only lead to resentment and burn-out.

My father used to tell me to go home at 5pm. 'Office hours are 9–5, outside of those hours you should be at home with your family.' Quite right, of course, but I had not reckoned on work being so addictive, especially for entrepreneurs. Where team members are working longer than reasonable hours then I think there is an obligation on other team members to find out what is wrong, and to offer support if needed.

A look at opposing Values

A person who had the opposite Values to us would be:

1 dishonest;

2 not accommodating of the needs of others;

3 lacking commitment to serving others;

4 unfair;

5 discourteous;

6 untrustworthy.

Realistically most people would not choose to work with someone who displayed any one of those Values! And yet in the business world we do come across people who are any or all of those things. Far too often we reluctantly accept poor quality or delivery of service. Or we feel we have no alternative but to work with someone who we do not trust. The question is – what can we do about it?

It is not always easy to assess whether a particular person is honest or dishonest, fair or unfair, courteous or discourteous – at least not on first meeting. What we can do, though, is get a sense of the person by reflection on these Values.

In the last part of this chapter I will explain how we assess people based on our Values, and then how we go about making changes to develop trust where none existed before. This process is an essential part of our business methods. We meet so many people who have been bruised by the antics of others. Their barriers are up. They are nervous, and as a defence present a strong façade. They can be demanding, or uncertain. They are not relaxed. It is part of our job to build trusting relationships – but we have to be realistic and recognise that we cannot do that with everyone.

Assessment

Our Values allow us to have an opinion of a tenant (and others) which relates to their behaviour. This beautifully undermines a common default position of valuing a tenant (and others) by how much they spend with us, how many employees they have, how big their business is, what kind of car they drive or just how loudly they shout at us. We are able to appreciate a tenant who is fair, courteous, trustworthy, and we can appreciate them with full understanding of what that means to us. Thus a tenant in a small unit with say two employees may get as much of our attention and service as a tenant in a larger unit, paying a much higher rent, and with a lot more employees.

Mutual trust

We know that our tenants trust us, and we know that we can trust them. This is the result of a long process of developing relationships by putting the Values into practice and finding that the tenants mirror those qualities. I used to be surprised that when I asked a tenant how they were doing in business they would tell me. They knew that I could use that information: to put up the rent if they were doing well, or try to get them out if they were not doing so well. But they told me because they trusted me not to do those things. And I never took advantage. To abuse trust is to destroy the relationship.

When Values are abused

When people abuse our Values by perhaps taking advantage of our good nature, then we:

- notice;
- tolerate (for a while);
- challenge (to give them a chance to understand us and change);
- and if necessary, take action.

It is a mistake for people to think that we don't notice their behaviour, and it is a mistake to think that we are an easy target because of our relaxed nature. Actually our Values give us great strength in our ability to assess when we are being abused and they give us a basis for a fair and sensible approach in doing something about it.

Sometimes poor behaviour that we have noticed in others is brought to our team meetings so that the team can all have a view on it and seek to understand. Eventually the behaviour is challenged by a team member. If there is no change of behaviour, even after a strong challenge, then we will find a way to stop working with that person, whoever they are. Usually this is a collective team decision. Interestingly, ejection of tenants does not happen often, they usually adapt their behaviour.

It is really important to understand that many rules and regulations are set up in order to prevent abuse. In my experience, rules are merely controls which close down the opportunity to build relationships. The controls affect all of our relationships and are an indication of a lack of trust. It is far better to implement a common sense regime to deal with abusers as they arise, rather than prevent abuses arising in the first place if it means displaying a general lack of trust in everyone. So my father's wise words – to extend trust to everyone – have now been slightly adapted. We extend trust to everyone, but carefully assess their resultant behaviour in order to establish whether we can build a relationship with them, or not. For the most part we can.

Anti-Value tenants

Mostly we assess prospective tenants or business introductions when we first meet them, so those who clearly do not share our Values are gently kept out of our network. But occasionally we have to take other action.

Arrogant. We had one tenant who was arrogant. His view was that he was always right. The team thought him to be sexist. There was no courtesy, no fairness, no basis for trust, and so there could be no connection. We decided we would tolerate his personality. Over time he has been fair and shown integrity in paying his rent, but still has a cold approach to relationships. So rather than eject him we use him as a learning exercise. It is a challenge to negotiate a rent review with him, but these challenges help us to grow, and by discussing what has happened with the team, all can benefit from the learning.

Lazy. In a similar example, our housekeeper suffered from tenants who would not wash up their own dirty mugs in the common kitchen. They would not even put the mugs in the dishwasher! The housekeeper felt she could not challenge this belittling behaviour. Instead she diffused her own stress by talking to the team and laughing about it. They identified the culprit and collectively and gently put pressure on him to change this behaviour which was more to do with laziness than arrogance.

Anti-Value tenants continued

Greedy. On one occasion we did eject a tenant. We had tolerated him for several years, and in that time while he had paid the rent, he had changed his company name several times. We realised that he was setting up businesses, building debts, then shutting down the business and starting again. The only reason someone does this is for their own personal greed and the belief that it is acceptable to take from others if he can get away with it. Not only do we choose not to work with anyone like that, we also do not want them on our Park. We refused to renew his lease.

Challenging others

One of the trickiest parts of the assessment process is what to do when someone tramples on our Values. We could choose to simply walk away – but that is doing nothing to help the other person. We could choose to challenge – but we fear that route in case our challenge is taken as criticism.

It is important to understand the difference between criticism and challenge. The first comes from judgement, and the second comes from a desire for improvement.

For example, if you have a poor service in a restaurant, what do you do? There are three choices.

- Do nothing. You don't want to cause a fuss.

- Complain. You want your money back.

- Challenge the quality. Explain why you were unhappy, but make it clear you are prepared to pay.

The first is unhelpful. Doing nothing comes from fear that you might be thought of as a critic and you might get into an argument. Or it comes from laziness – why bother? But you probably would not return to that restaurant, and you would probably tell lots of people about the poor service.

The second comes from knowing your 'rights' and demanding reparations are made. It is an understandable extension of the belief that everything in life, including buying a meal, is a contract. However, it is selfish and it stems from perfectionism and ego.

The third comes from a desire to help the restaurant improve – it is a gift. A good business owner will always appreciate feedback given with good intent. We can all learn through practice to give a challenge generously, and receive one with grace.

Breaking the resistance to challenging each other

Once I understood the process above, then I had to find a way to break the barrier of resistance to challenging each other, and I did this in two ways.

Firstly I was prepared myself to challenge poor behaviour, and to praise behaviour in line with our Values, and in each case state why it was poor or good behaviour – which Value was being trodden on or adhered to.

Secondly I facilitated a team meeting where we could work out between ourselves the difference between challenge and criticism.

The conclusion of this team meeting was that the way you challenge, and the way you receive a challenge are fundamentally important. The two elements are linked. For everyone giving a challenge, another person is receiving it. In receiving a challenge the team feedback was that they often felt belittled or embarrassed. They perhaps should have known better, and they take it personally. Also they can get angry and then fight back by blaming or being defensive (toxic responses which undermine relationships and strengthen inequality). We agreed that a better response is to accept the challenge, and be curious about it.

We agreed that it is a good idea when challenged to sleep on it, and to talk to someone about it to get a balanced view.

To challenge someone takes courage. You are facing up to the possibility of a response as outlined above. But now we know the response that is possible, the fear of challenging someone is lessened. We can challenge with care and help the person recognise that the challenge is not meant as criticism, but as a point of learning.

We started to practise challenge, and praise, on each other in the team so that we could gauge reactions and build confidence before trying it out on our tenants. As each new member of the team sees this happening, they also learn to emulate the same behaviours.

When someone challenges you, seek first to understand how they are trying to help you improve, rather than assuming they are being critical and jumping to a defensive mode.

Our Values give us a basis for good behaviour towards others and also give us a solid platform on which to challenge behaviour of others. Through that process we can build relationships based on equality, respect and independence.

For my part, I consider it an honour when I am challenged by anyone that they have taken the time to make me think and question my behaviour or actions. We all need these checks and balances. We are all fallible. We are all susceptible to the growth of our ego. Challenges keep me grounded.

The growth of self-confidence

Looking back now at this process through my life, I realise that standing up for my Values was a big factor in the growth of my own self-confidence, and I think it has done the same for every member of the team. The commercial property industry is quite a masculine industry driven by capital investment returns and 'professional' services. It does not have to be like that. Bringing my Values into the industry meant being accepting of others judging me for being different. It was hard, and I felt weak, vulnerable, 'less than' the others in the industry. But now that we have built up an exceptional team, who think and act in the same way, it is so much easier.

The team hold the same Values, and tenants and providers think and act the in same way. The culture is very strong.

I have come to realise that real strength is not in our ability to control a situation, real strength comes from our ability to trust. Real wealth emanates from the same place. Real wealth is having a fulfilling and happy life filled with people you want around you. And this is just as much true in business is it is in family life.

CHAPTER NINE

Overlaying
Purpose

―――――

Understanding why we do
what we do

> **I learned this, at least, by my experiment:**
> **that if one advances confidently in the direction**
> **of his dreams, and endeavours to live the life**
> **which he has imagined, he will meet with a**
> **success unexpected in common hours.**

Henry David Thoreau –
Life in the Woods

It is often assumed that the reason we work hard is in order to fulfil our need to generate income. This begs the question: 'At what point does a job become motivational beyond the salary?'

There have been plenty of studies that show that incentivising by bonus or by promise of a higher salary works to a point, and then stops working. It is a short-term fix. When we have sufficient, we do not need more, and will not work harder or longer hours in order to earn more.

Furthermore if a team member is motivated to continuously make more money, then they are working for themselves, self-serving. They are not working for you or for the team, except incidentally. Such people can be disruptive in a team.

Earning a salary is a means to an end, not an end in itself.

We earn the money so that we can do something with it. Having covered the basics – food, clothing, shelter – we then get to choose what we really want to do and the money helps us in that process.

In our search for meaning in life (see *Man's Search for Meaning* by Victor Frankl) we need to earn sufficient to live, but earning should never be a substitute for finding and doing what fulfils us, what makes us happy, what gives us hope, or what makes our heart sing.

These things can be found in Purpose. Typically Purpose is about doing something for others, or righting a wrong. We begin to realise that serving ourselves is ultimately a lonely activity. Purpose, in contrast, is social in nature. Purpose is perhaps the justification why many people choose to go into public service, or to work for a charity.

- I believe that everyone has an underlying Purpose, a reason for being.

- I believe that our whole life, and all our experiences, shift us towards our Purpose, whether we know it or not.

- I believe Purpose is what makes us human. Purpose is what makes our lives fulfilling.

Most people are so caught up in the struggle to live, that they do not actively seek their own Purpose in life. I am constantly surprised how many people accept a job that they dislike, but do it anyway because they need the money. The higher the pay, the more people become trapped.

Some find their Purpose in a hobby, or by volunteering. Some have a job which inspires them because it is in line with their Purpose, and it is both motivating and fulfilling and a pleasure to work hard at it. Some seem to think that life is about making money. They never find a true Purpose, or perhaps they believe that making money and owning material things is their Purpose.

All of the above applies to an individual, but it is also true of a business.

Why do people start a business?

There are three basic reasons why a person decides to start a business.

To make a living. Clearly for a business owner it is imperative to be able to earn sufficient to 'feed, clothe, and house themselves and their family'. This is no different than the employee wanting to earn enough to cover life's basic costs. Once the basic income is generated, then the owner can think beyond income. Initially that may mean emotional needs, such as feelings of accomplishment, and beyond that we start to think about what fulfils us. This was famously espoused by Abraham Maslow in 1943 in his Hierarchy of Needs.

To be independent. In my experience of talking to thousands of business owners what really motivates them is the desire for independence. Most people start a business to get away from the frustrations of employment.

Running your own business gives you the freedom to make your own mind up what you do, when you do it, how you do it, who you work with and where you work.

These are key drivers for people who run their own business.

To pursue a passion. Everyone who starts a business works on something that they are especially good at, or passionate about. To be able to do something that you love, and you know makes a difference in the world, that is where true passion emanates from, and that is what motivates us to work hard, even for little financial reward.

I believe the greatest of the three is the third. To run a business is to follow your passion for what you want to do with your life. Therein lies your Purpose, the reason why you run the business.

The Great Lie in business is that we are led to believe that people run a business solely in order to maximise profit, as though we are all driven by personal greed.

This has arisen because we equate business activity with what we hear in the news, and that is all about large corporations, where there is a separation of ownership and control, and a focus on making money.

But the Great Lie leads many people to accept competition, control and abuse as normal in business. It follows that there are people out there who think it is okay to take from the business owner, and accordingly business owners who accept their lot as the abused party.

Purpose then is hugely important. Being able to focus on why you are in business is very powerful, and is the mark of an authentic leader. When you are able with confidence to be able to say 'this is why we do it', that is a clear statement that contradicts the assumptions of others that 'you are only in it to make as much money as possible'. Clarity of Purpose is the difference between engendering trust because you are being clear about your motives, and tolerating an assumption of distrust because with no expression of an alternative, people will assume you only care about what you can gain for yourself.

The importance of Purpose

In his book *Outwitting the Devil*, Napoleon Hill talks about two ways of living which he calls drifting and decisiveness. People who drift have no clear purpose to their lives. People who are decisive know what they want because they know why they are doing it.

In my experience the majority of business owners do have a passion for their work. The problem is that many do not know how to translate that into a clear Purpose. It is one thing I have realised, to act according to your own sense of Purpose, it is another thing altogether to communicate to others why you are doing what you do.

If your team see you as a drifter, then they will drift through lack of leadership. This is how lack of Purpose stifles growth. However, if the leader is decisive, following a clear Purpose, then the team will aspire to follow.

Deciding Purpose

In the course of running my family business, I began to realise that I did not make decisions based purely on maximising profit, but on building relationships. I could not make a decision to make profit if at the same time it caused offence to anyone. I am not a purely profit-orientated businessman.

Having established the Values, which focused the team behaviour, I recognised the need to establish a Purpose, in order to build team direction – so that we are all headed on the same path.

We would be a business not merely set up to make money, but also to show consideration and respect for the people who work with us.

It was not easy to work out our Purpose; I mulled it over for some years. I would have to communicate it to the team, and beyond. What if I set the wrong Purpose? The fear of what others think of us is an expression of the need for approval, and running a business does not make this fear disappear. I knew I could not bring myself to make money at the expense of someone else, or if it damaged the environment. Money-making for me had to be accompanied by consideration of the needs of others.

I considered how I felt about each group of stakeholders in the business. What do they really value about being part of the business.

- The acid test for our tenants (over and above having good premises, a fair rent and a landlord who treats them well) is – do I feel valued and cared about? If so, then there is little reason to leave and every reason to talk about how great the landlord is.

- The acid test (over and above having a stable job with a good salary and an understanding boss) for the team member is – do I feel valued and can I grow as part of a team which is united in a strong sense of wanting to do some good?

- The acid test for the shareholders (over and above a financial return on investment) is – can we accept the Purpose and still make money while at the same time feeling content that our investment is being put to good use? Here I am blessed with an understanding family with shared Values.

The point is that while our focus is on valuing people, the expected outcome is still to make money.

I began to realise that valuing people is what I have always done, balancing respect for them with the stakeholders' needs.

So the Purpose emerged: 'To create an environment where people feel valued'.

Understanding our Purpose

Our Purpose is not about *making* someone feel valued. That is not possible. Instead we create the environment where people *can work it out for themselves* that we value them. That is an important distinction, and worthy of some explanation.

To value someone is:

- to show that you care about them;
- to treat them as an equal, and to respect them for who they are;
- to recognise that they can contribute;
- to help them attain and retain their independence in thought and deed as far as possible, and certainly not to exert your own power over them;
- to extend our Values to them without attachment to those Values being reciprocated.

I hope it is clear that our Purpose is therefore Social. I guess this makes Jennings a Social Enterprise. That does not mean that we are not intending to make a profit. It just means that we are a profit-making organisation that has a Social Purpose at heart so while some of our profit is distributed to shareholders, most of it is ploughed back into pursuing the Purpose. As we grow the business, so we grow the Purpose. And as we become successful we are able to show that a Purpose-driven business is able to make a profit, but as an outcome rather than as an objective. And finally the better we become at delivering the Purpose, the easier it is to make a profit.

Social enterprise

It is perhaps useful to note at this point that in my view charities and businesses are slowly merging together under the heading of Social Enterprise. As charities are experiencing funding cuts, so they are having to find other ways to generate income – in other words they are becoming enterprising. As business culture is changing, so business owners are finding that they have to be less profit-focused and more community-minded in order to maintain long-term viability. The meeting point is an enterprise with a Social Purpose.

Introducing Purpose

The first step of working with Purpose is to communicate it to the team. I think it helped that my attitude in running the business had always been Purpose-led, I just didn't realise it.

My Purpose-led approach

- From the start, I have only ever employed people who have no experience in the commercial property industry because I knew I needed people who would look after my tenants, not focus on the buildings alone.

- I was careful to appoint a gardening contractor who would plant only indigenous species. I want the Park to remain a rural environment where people work, rather than a business park that looks pristine. I value the natural environment in which we all work.

- Rather than requiring formal references for prospective tenants, I would look them in the eye and shake their hand. That is the truth that I told another property owner when he asked me what references I requested. He was suitably shocked (well, that probably was my intention!). I extended trust. I value the relationship over and above the legal niceties.

- I sought to minimise the formal paperwork, limiting licence agreements to one page and leases to four pages, written in plain English. I value the tenants' time and money.

- Rent reviews became an excuse for a coffee and a chat with a friend about what incoming tenants were paying for similar premises. Being greedy, or thought to be greedy, would undermine the relationship. Being fair strengthens the relationship. Judging the difference is the hard part. I value the relationship.

What I needed to do was to create a framework so that I could delegate decision-making to the team. But I could not delegate authority and responsibility if the team did not fully understand where their authority came from, and what they were responsible to – the Purpose. Without a definitive statement of Purpose, the default is the assumption that the right decision is one which minimises costs and/or maximises income.

The strength to deflect doubt

I knew that there would be many detractors, not so much within the team, but outside influencers. It is so easy to fall into the trap of accepting and adapting to what we assume others think of us. It is important to keep away from such influences. To declare that the Purpose is not to focus on money is to step outside of the assumptive norm of maximising profit.

So it is not good enough to merely understand the Purpose, we have to be strong enough that we can deflect any doubters.

Maintaining focus

I first introduced our Purpose to the team at a team meeting and it followed on logically from their acceptance of Values. Once adopted, we need to keep our focus, which we do in a number of ways:

- by communicating Purpose (and Values) regularly, in order to attract those who accept and understand our position, and keep away those that do not;
- by constantly communicating within the team by team meetings and coaching;

Doubters come in many forms

- A team member who holds on to, or reverts back to, the belief that they may advance their career if they show they have made money for the company.

- A team member who slips back into making unreasonable demands of tenants, unconsciously exerting their power and denting the relationship in doing so.

- Professional advisors assuming that your aim is to maximise income and giving advice accordingly.

- Professionals seeking to minimise your risks and leading you into contractual arrangements which can undermine your Purpose.

Choose staff and professional advisors well.
Make sure they understand you.

- by constantly checking in on ourselves that our decisions are in line with Purpose.

In addition, all new team members are inducted into working with Purpose.

Purpose as a basis for decisions

Purpose is the one key factor that underpins all of our decisions. It is not acceptable to make a decision which undermines our Purpose.

Having said that, rarely is a decision made that affects only one aspect of the business. We do need to retain a balance between the requirement to follow our Purpose and the financial impact on the company. A negative financial impact is not necessarily a problem if it is small, whereas clearly a decision in line with Purpose which bankrupts the company does nothing to further our Purpose in the long term! The business must be financially sustainable. There needs to be balance.

With this understanding all the team are able to take responsibility for their own decisions, and they can be confident in being accountable with honesty and transparency.

After all how can a decision made 'on Purpose' be a mistake? Through this process, individual self-confidence grows. Team members become confident in their decisions, and as that happens so managers can let go of decision-making. This is the start of the transition from management to leadership. We lead the way and allow the team to run the business within the constructs of the Purpose and the Values. Our team leaders then start to look beyond the business for opportunities to develop and grow the business. It is a win-win situation.

Purpose is motivational

As our team have gelled together, they have become tribal. They support each other. When one is struggling, the others will step in to help. They volunteer willingly. They work long hours when needed and take time off when they need it. They want to come to work and they have fun while at work. They understand that there is no pressure on them to maximise profits for the sake of building the wealth of the shareholders. Instead we are together building an organisation which values each other in the team as equals, and we value our customers and suppliers as equals too. As the business grows, so does their part in it and their income from it.

Purpose and power

Our Purpose allows us to work out where the balance of power is in our relationships with others. Relationships vary between the two extremes of 'exerting power' to 'being subservient'. Balance is where we do not exert our power as landlords over tenants, as managers over junior staff, as payers over providers. Equally balance is where we do not allow ourselves to be subservient to our customers, our managers, or our professionals. Everybody is valued as an equal. We all have the opportunity to say what we think in the knowledge that our opinion will be valued. That is our Purpose.

Our Purpose is a tool for building relationships. There is no doubt that if you value people, then over the long term the relationship will prove fruitful and profit will grow as an outcome, without it having to be an objective.

Mission and vision statements

Lots of businesses, and especially larger ones, have a mission statement, or a vision statement. These are not the same thing as Purpose. They are statements of what you *do*, or where you expect to be going with what you *do*. A good example is a Formula 1 racing team whose reputed mission is 'does it make the car go faster?' One could argue that this is the Purpose of the business, but I would suggest that this is what the business does, not *why* it does it.

No-lease tenancy

I did consider once whether we should run a business park without contracts. A no-lease tenancy. That would be a first, I think, for commercial property (at least as a deliberate policy). After all, a lease contract can be construed as an indication that you do not trust your tenant, and at the very least that you do not value them except as conduits of financial return. Is a lease then against our Purpose? I came to the conclusion that a good lease works for both parties as confirmation of an agreement. Transparency (Honesty and Openness) is the key factor here. There is nothing to hide because the agreement is amicable to both parties because it is based on Fairness. So the lease remains in place.

Quite often mission and vision statements are contrived to motivate a large team. Businesses will spend large amounts with coaches who come up with some bland statement for mission or vision. This is communicated to the staff and then promptly ignored by everyone. It will probably be written on a wall somewhere, and written into the Annual Report and Accounts, but essentially it is a meaningless exercise. Even if it had meaning, it would be limited to *what* they do. There is no inspiration in such statements.

A vision can only work effectively in a business if the team members sign up to it, if they share the vision. But the vision is usually merely a statement of how big the organisation could be, and few people can be inspired by that.

Purpose is different.

Purpose is a statement of *why* you do it. The why can be shared by the whole team. They can buy in to it. It is difficult to work out your Purpose, especially for larger businesses where the profit motive is so ingrained. We are so used to telling the story of what we do, that we forget or ignore why we do it. Used properly, the Purpose is a platform for authoritative decision-making for everyone. Purpose therefore leads to freedom.

Purpose undermines hierarchical structure, control and power-mongering. Purpose makes it possible to have a flat structure, where everyone in the business can be innovative and lead on a task. Purpose therefore leads to equality.

When you work out the Purpose for your business, don't write it on the wall; communicate it and live it so that your team can buy into it.

I realise that very few businesses follow a Purpose beyond profit. It is rare, it is precious and we must nurture it. Purpose is a driver for change. In fact it is the driver for change in our growing experience of a new culture emerging out of the devastation being wrought by the profit-mongers.

We must remember that money is just a tool, a means to an end but not an end in itself.

Money is not the root of all evil; the love of money is the root of all evil (Timothy 6:10). Setting a Purpose puts the love for something else above the love for money.

Inauthentic Purpose

For me, Purpose is something that a person wishes to attain that is beyond their need for material things, something which is personally fulfilling. For a business, Purpose is beyond profit-making. While profit-making is important, Purpose is what inspires, motivates and unites the business owner and the team.

As Purpose in business becomes more commonplace, be aware of those who will misunderstand the concept. They will try to say that they are a Purposeful company. But actions speak louder than words. Doing something to benefit your community is meaningless if at the same time your behaviour to your team or your suppliers is repugnant.

Watch out for business support organisations and consultants purporting to offer advice on Purpose, but whose underlying belief stems from their assumption of the need for businesses to maximise profit. To operate purposefully, businesses have to drop the concept of maximising profit and think of profit as an outcome. For many businesses, especially larger ones, this will be virtually impossible to achieve.

It is important to recognise that Values represent common behaviour, and Purpose represents direction. The two work together, not in isolation. A Purpose which undermines our common Values is inauthentic. Permitting your team to make decisions on Purpose, without taking account of the agreed Values, is undermining and will damage the team unity. My own view is that Values should be agreed first, and then Purpose is overlaid so that the agreed behaviours find a direction that motivates all team members.

How to find your Purpose

As I have said, finding your Purpose is not easy and you will need to dig deep.

Look first for anything to do with community or of a social nature, where humanity is being advanced.

Secondly look back to your childhood. Sometimes we have a driving need to heal what hurt us in childhood, to right a wrong.

Thirdly look to what you are passionate about, what really drives you, and/or what you find fulfilling.

I have been helping others with Purpose and here are some examples:

- **For a dance instructor.** To help young teenagers grow in self-confidence and self-belief through the medium of dance.

- **For a personal trainer.** To be able to support and encourage effort. This person felt the lack of encouragement she had as a child and was determined to give her best in this way to any of her customers.

- **For a team coach.** To build equality in team cultures. This person has felt inequality in her past and decided to make it her life's ambition to do something about it.

In each case, the Purpose is something deeper and more important than making money. However, making money is essential in order to keep delivering the Purpose, and the more money you make, the more resource you can drive into the Purpose.

For each of the above examples as they grow the business their major issue would be the need to communicate their Purpose with confidence and by doing that attract to them people who understand and embrace the Purpose. In this way the Purpose grows.

From a wider viewpoint and from experience of our tenants I have found that engineers who run businesses are usually focused on the design and usefulness of their product, rather than sales. We have three teachers who started a business because they saw a need for better 3D printing machines in schools. We have furniture manufacturers who got fed up with mass-produced product and wanted to focus on bespoke furniture, which is more of a challenge to produce and therefore more fulfilling. The point is that in every case profit is not the prime motivator. However, they all understand that without making a profit they cannot grow the business and further the Purpose.

CHAPTER TEN

Introduction to **Principles**

Opening up the way to
individual self-development

Bricks and mortar sing us no audible tune, the heart opens only to the human chant of being.

Pramahansa Yogananda –
Autobiography of a Yogi

I think it is fair to say that Purpose was the missing link. We had embedded the Values as a team, and our joint behaviour had gelled really well. Everybody in the team understands the Values and makes every effort to comply with them, and not abuse them. We all do this naturally and with pleasure and ease.

Purpose added the extra dimension that frees up the team members to be generous where that is a way to make someone feel valued and to build loyalty, and just because it is the right thing to do.

We had implemented a culture where:

- in making our decisions we would first consider a Purpose beyond making profit;
- in our behaviour we would use mutually agreed Values as a basis for putting people before profit.

But I was beginning to feel that this was not sufficient. I felt the need to invest more detail in what it means to work with an ethical culture. This led to the establishment of 18 Principles intended to add guidance to the team. The Principles are explained in more detail in the Appendix.

The Principles are grouped under three broad headings: Team, Purpose and Community and in this chapter I want to explain how these work at Jennings.

Team

One of the key elements of any business is the need to distribute tasks amongst the team. No matter what the business does, someone has to do every job that needs doing. And that means that someone has to manage the allocation of tasks: a manager.

And herein lies a problem because for a manager the easiest way to allocate tasks is to point and direct. 'Do this task in this way'. This method of managing is depressing. It kills innovation. It shows no leadership skills, and it implies a lack of care in the development of team members. It is only about getting a job done. In my view this control style of management comes from fear. And the karmic effect is that this method limits the personal growth of the manager, who will spend all their time managing and monitoring, and therefore not learning.

Opportunity

The principle of Opportunity, focuses on this area. Every team member is given an opportunity when they work for us. They will normally be employed for a particular role, but that quickly develops as they are encouraged to do tasks which are outside their comfort zone. This can happen in various ways. For a junior person it may be to create a spreadsheet for a particular purpose or to attend a business networking meeting . For another, it could be to develop a plan and deliver a project. I am proud to say that every member of our team has advanced in their role from when they started. We have been able to attract job applicants with good attitude who share our Values, encourage them to join us, develop their potential by affording them opportunities, and promote them to positions of responsibility – all in the space of a few years.

The natural flow of accepting, learning and passing on a task

Sometimes we stand back in amazement at the quality of work produced and the innovative ways in which our team members tackle a task presented to them. A good example is of our quarterly newsletter Park Bench, which goes out to over 1,000 people in our community. In the past eight years no less than four different team members have had the job of editor, and each editor morphs the publication into something better.

At the same time each editor has gained experience of:

- enlisting the support of the previous editor;
- having authority over the article writers (I even get bullied on this!);
- dealing with printers (providers) and having authority over the quality;
- dealing with distribution and feedback;
- leading on a task, without the comfort of being managed;
- delivering on a project and feeling proud of the outcome;
- gracefully receiving praise for a job well done;
- letting go of the task to the next team member to take on the role;
- and offering support to the next editor.

Change and continual improvement, failure and praise

Our principle of Change plays into this arena. We expect not only for a team member to be up for the challenge of a new task, but we expect them also to own the task. In other words, we would explain the desired outcome but not the route. This gives each team member the Responsibility and Authority to get on with it in their own way. Thus they can take the lead on change.

We embrace change and we try not to dictate, so that in everything we do there is a possibility for improvement. The principle of Continual Improvement addresses this.

The action of asking someone in the team to try something new to them has to come with three caveats.

1   Firstly we have to offer them our full support in the task being proffered. Support does not mean doing the task, watching over them or micro-managing them. Support means being available if the recipient needs help or clarity.

2   Secondly we have to embrace failure as a team. Sometimes the team member will make a hash of it. We have to understand, support and encourage rather than criticise. We expect the team member to be honest around failure, and we expect to use the experience as a basis for all team members to learn. No one in the team has made as many, or bigger mistakes, than I have. I am the king of mistakes. Communicating that message offers relief to those who are anxious around failure.

> **Failure is not the issue. What we learn from failure makes us better.**

3   Thirdly, and sitting closely alongside failure, is the importance of praise for a job well done. It shows care and consideration. While I am not so good at this, I have noticed that there are some in the team who are exceptional in their praise-giving abilities.

Few things are as motivational as a pat on the back, a sign of appreciation.

We would do well to remember that we are all equally capable of supporting, failing and praising.

Delegation

Delegation has become much easier now that we all have the awareness from the Values, the Purpose and the Principles. We now delegate with trust rather than with control. There is no longer a need to micro-manage to make sure the job is done properly. Our form of delegation is one of readily 'letting go' of a task to someone else, with care, with support if needed, and with trust that they will do the task to the best of their abilities and ask if they get stuck.

Our approach is designed to minimise the fear attached to taking on new challenges.

As long as the Values are adhered to, and the Purpose is uppermost in their thoughts, then each team member has little to fear. There is always the anxiety around 'what if I make a mistake?', but self-confidence comes only when you have begun to conquer your self-doubts.

By delegating tasks, we help our team members to believe in their abilities, and they become much more competent and confident people as a result. At the same time, team members who take on new roles help by freeing up the managers from any attachment to their roles.

Attachment to roles is such a negative vibe in a business environment. It used to have a name – demarcation. Attachment holds back a business from the opportunities to develop and to innovate. Passing on a role gives both an opportunity for the recipient to develop a new skill, and for the giver to free up some time to find something else to do.

And let's not run away with the idea that this has to be a top-down process. While it is true that the giver helps the recipient by offering them an opportunity, it also works the other way round. The recipient can help the giver by relieving them of a task they need not be doing. This can happen where a more junior person in the team is more outgoing, adaptable and optimistic, and their line manager is perhaps more nervous of change and wants to hold on to the task. The junior person can activate delegation by identifying the task and volunteering for it.

At Jennings, we have seen all of this in action. The beauty of it is that both the manager and the junior can effect change in each other and, of course, the pay-off is growth. Or to put it another way, to hang on to your roles prevents both the growth of the organisation and your own personal growth.

Purpose

Our Purpose is: 'To create an environment where people feel valued'. We cannot make people feel valued, we can only create an environment that makes it possible for people to feel valued. We do that with our attitude. It is important to note that this is profit neutral: our attitude is the way we behave and it is no way linked to whether we make a profit or not. In a business world fixated on the profit imperative it is important to communicate Purpose with resolve, encouraging all team members to use Purpose as a basis for decision-making, rather than the more base desire to maximise profit.

The general principles of Empathy, Courtesy, Generosity and Kindness give basic guidance for showing respect to another person no matter who they are. I could add forgiveness and tolerance as well! These concepts are imperative in showing that we value another person. We need to have them uppermost in our mind in all our relationships.

Where we are collectively, as a team, showing others that we value them through our thoughts, words and deeds, then we are expressing the Purpose of the business. But remember, as I have said, we have to balance the need to make a profit against the need to follow our Purpose, and we have to balance the desire to control so that no one can take advantage of our good nature, with the need to free people to own their behaviour because that makes them feel valued. Balance can be established by reference to Fairness.

Generally speaking, when we empathise, show courtesy, express generosity and extend kindness, these attributes are appreciated and reciprocated. It makes us feel good. It is fulfilling. It motivates us to build relationships and it builds trust. And trust builds business.

Community

One of the issues with Purpose is to be aware that it is so easy to slide back to the old methods of running a business – the 'for maximum profit no matter the consequences' business. And so we have to be diligent at all times. The second set of principles highlights some ways in which our culture can be undermined.

Pay attention to the facilities

When considering the environment in which others feel valued, we must pay attention to our facilities as well as our behaviour. Facilities do not have to be pristine. They have to be comfortable and functional, and we have to be aware of our customers' needs and accommodate them if that is sensible. If we slip in our attention to caring about our environment, then we are not valuing other users of our environment. I remember when my father walked round the Park, he would always keep one eye on the ground in front, and on many occasion I saw him stoop to pick up a nail. His comment was – 'that could end up in someone's tyre'. Even now I notice those who are aware of their environment, those who will stoop to pick up rubbish. It is an action which expresses that we value others. Also if we make the facilities too pristine, we create a false and uncomfortable working environment. It is rather like taking your young children to visit an extraordinarily tidy aunt. If an environment is too pristine we have a child-like fear of damaging it.

Be careful with recommendations

We must be ultra-careful in endorsing others, for to endorse or recommend is to give a seal of approval by which others will judge us against our Values. Endorsement to an untrustworthy person will undermine our Values. It is for this reason that we are very selective who we invite to speak at our network events. We have a rule that they must never promote themselves, but instead they are there to gift some knowledge or experience. Just being there is an acknowledgement that we endorse them. Sponsorship is a form of endorsement. On one occasion we sponsored the local Business Awards. It did not sit well with us. We are not comfortable with this kind of self-promotion. We agreed to sponsor for one year on the basis that they added an Ethical Business of the Year Award. That award was dropped the following year. Perhaps we were ahead of our time.

Avoid grants

We avoid seeking grants of any sort. It may seem extreme to not wish to take free money, but I am well aware that there is actually no such thing as free money. Grants tend to have strings attached, which can easily pull us away from our Purpose. Grants are also very frustrating. We had one occasion where there was an unnecessary and unexpected delay caused by the grant-giver's bureaucratic process which had severe knock-on effects to the business. If you are offered a grant, be very aware of the rules surrounding it and do not get sucked in to do too much work when there is little chance of success.

The Principles are set out in more detail in The Appendix for those who want to read more.

CHAPTER ELEVEN

A Culture
Emerges

———

Recognising the tipping point
into a new culture

Every newly made acquaintanceship between people ripens into friendship and then into spiritual harmony (sometimes called love) or plants a germ of suspicion and doubt which evolves and grows into open rebellion, according to the way in which participants in the acquaintanceship relate themselves to one another.

Napoleon Hill –
Outwitting the Devil

Running a business, trying to be strong and show self-confidence, and all the while being full of self-doubt and uncertainty, has not been easy. The accountant in me urged caution and protection. The rebel in me wanted to push the boundaries and stand out. My natural ability to trust people was sometimes abused and left me feeling vulnerable. I knew I could erect barriers to prevent that abuse, or I could find a way to avoid the abusers so that I could extend trust with confidence. I chose the latter.

During this journey I have resolved a few issues that plagued me. I now know:

- that the majority of people returned my trust in them, and appreciated it. Not many took advantage of me. It is just that each one that did had quite a big emotional impact;
- how to tolerate those who show no gratitude for the trust extended;
- when and how to let go of those I choose not to work with;
- how to build a team that is also able to do those things;
- that the team is at the heart of any business, and where growth either emanates or suffocates;
- that running a business is an emotional journey of discovery much more than it is one of personal financial gain.

Understanding the above has led me to appreciate that trust is a fundamental basis for good business. Control is the antithesis of trust. To trust without control, and to do nothing to dent other people's trust in you is, in my view, the basis for a culture shift.

The process of establishing Values and Purpose at Jennings afforded us a platform to focus our attention on behaviour, rather than on moneymaking. It meant giving ourselves permission to let go of customers, staff and contractors who do not share our Values. It changed our attitude from the need to win, to being prepared only to work with people who would appreciate us for what we stand for, who we are – our Values.

There were no role models, no one to emulate. We just did what we felt was right.

That is not to say that others have not been thinking in the same way. I could name several enterprises in Oxfordshire alone that are working out new cultures in different ways but with the common theme of doing good in and for our community, and treating their teams with the respect they deserve.

In the academic world there are also many advocates of new cultures. Take a look at the *Ted Talk* video *Start with Why?* by Simon Sinek (www.ted.com). In it he explains that a business can be segregated by the *What?*, the *How?* and the *Why?* of business. Every business knows *What* they do; few start with *Why* they do it. *Why* is your Purpose, your reason for doing *What* you do, your reason for getting up in the morning, where the passion and enthusiasm comes from. Not many business owners even think about it but, as Simon says, the most inspired businesses understand their Purpose. Where I differ from Simon is that he skips over the *How*, implying that the *How* is part of the process, the link between *Why* and *What*. For me the *How* is your collective chosen behaviour and that is neatly embedded in our Values and enhanced by our Principles.

I would also direct you to three authors who have a good understanding of leadership in this arena: Seth Godin, Robin Sharma and Robert Rabbin.

While the culture we have developed has emanated from our Values and Purpose, I think it is worth taking a quick look at some of the key elements in the ongoing process.

The tipping point // from management by control to leadership with trust

It has been an interesting exercise to look back at the process that we have been through and recognise that there was a tipping point in the team. Before we reached that point, most were sceptical about the Values and whether it would be possible to collectively operate from a values perspective. It is easy to be critical in the face of the expectation of the 'business is business' majority.

Once we reached the tipping point the majority of the team had taken the Values to heart and begun to operate from them. They had accepted the culture, and were now ready to develop it, with less input from me.

We are well past that point now.

We have a superb team of confident and independent individuals who are able to be themselves at work. Through their differences they are able to complement each other because the underlying Values that we share bind us as a team.

Furthermore the team members are now developing their own ideas from the culture, stretching the boundaries in ways I could never have imagined. Recently the team, led by Chris, put together a beautifully crafted document which is our Staff Handbook (how many business owners can proudly talk about their staff handbook being 'beautifully crafted'?). I am so proud of them for this achievement. It is a far better job than I could have done. When we give this handbook to new employees, it is a statement of how we work, with simplicity and clarity, accepting the regulations where they are sensible, and keeping everything else succinct and simple. Contrast this short handbook to the reams of pages of legally drawn-up policy documents that some new employees have to sign – it must be quite scary. Our handbook is an exemplar of how Openness and Honesty helps to diminish fear and uncertainty.

My point is that the team members are united now in their ability to enhance our systems and processes in ways which add to the culture rather than ways which drag us back to the old methods of management by control. In this approach each one of the team is innovative and uses their initiative.

Simply copying what others do is the road back to mediocrity.

It is a credit to Paul's leadership that these processes flourish rather than flounder.

There is also a tipping point in relation to working with others outside the team. Where the majority of our customers respond to our behaviour and reciprocate, then we can more easily spot those who do not. And then we can with confidence challenge poor attitude with clarity and honesty, and without attachment. This applies equally to providers. Through this process the culture that we have built as a team is extended out to all our relationships.

Marketing by attraction // communication rather than promotion

Another thing that I am proud of is the way in which we do our marketing. I well remember those days back in 1991 when I tried a postal mailshot to rent out some of our newly converted office premises. I had the tricky problem of how to engage business owners at the time they were considering moving premises – a virtually impossible task. And, of course, I suffered from the lack of interest from the commercial agents. That would be the traditional route to market in our industry, but it does not work as well if you are trying to let very small business units to start-up businesses in a rural area.

We knew that most people made a decision on premises based primarily on location and price. How could we get them to consider us and our more holistic approach?

The way we did it was by getting out of the office and communicating – networking. As the team grew, we encouraged all of them to do it. Networking is a brilliant opportunity for inexperienced staff to get out of the office and simply enthuse about their job. Some learned to stand up and talk (one-minute presentations) for the first time at these events. They are great for building personal self-confidence. At the same time as they are facing their fears, and building their confidence, team members would also be representing the company and all that we stand for. This then is a perfect way to do something for our staff, and also to trust them to be able to enthuse about the business in front of other business owners and professionals.

Our objective is to let as many people as possible know about who we are, where we are, what we do and what we stand for.

There is never any attempt to sell, just to communicate, and allow others to decide to come and visit us. This process is now rolled up into our Principle of 'Marketing by Attraction rather than Promotion'.

We don't sell. We communicate with enthusiasm for what we do and pride in how we do it, in order to provide people with the option to buy.

This process has worked well for us. We recognise that everyone is a potential marketer.

Everyone in our team, every customer, every provider and every local person whose life we have touched in one way or another is a potential marketer for our business.

Our business is growing because of our reputation for fairness and trust. What I started out believing to be possible has now come to fruition and is working in our favour. Our reputation goes out into our community far beyond what a commercial agent could do for us. As a result, our premises are never empty for very long, and that means that we are more profitable and without the expense of agency fees.

Crucially, and I hope this is clear by now, profit is an outcome of treating people properly rather than an objective.

Dealing with events outside our control //
embracing change

The team now decide who they want to work with. Their decision is based on whether they believe they can build a relationship with them or not. I have already explained that they do the recruitment of new team members, and that they effectively 'interview' prospective tenants. This process puts attitude above aptitude every time. The contract (lease or employment contract) and the money (rent or salary) are kept very much in the background. But it is not always straightforward.

Sometimes events happen where we have no choice over the participants. One such event is worth explaining. We leased some premises in a nearby town, and sub-divided the offices to be let to about 30 individual small businesses. Our landlord was a corporate business and the local director we dealt with was a good man.

The lease was coming to an end and we had assumed that it would simply be renewed. However, the local director had retired and the landlord's agent had other ideas. At first they would not communicate with us. Our letters and emails six months before the lease end were ignored. Phone messages left with the agent's secretary were not returned. With about two months before the end of the lease, one of my team (out of exasperation) contacted another leaseholder of the property and found out that they had done a deal with the agent to take over our space. They needed our space, but did not need all of it. They then had the arrogance to assume that we would continue to rent from them the space that they did not need – and at double the rent! The team were mortified and quite severely knocked back by this turn of events. It was so deceitful, and so against our Values, so selfish and uncaring.

I should point out here that both the agent and the other leaseholder would probably not have thought they were doing anything wrong – it was just business to them. The issue was not with the outcome, but with the lack of communication so that we could not give our tenants more time to find alternative premises.

We had to let our tenants know what had happened, why it had happened, why we had not been able to give them any decent notice, and what their options were. We had to give them the choices based on the truth. It was most important that we communicated that we had not been part of this, and that we too had been shafted by the antics of the agent, whose name I am sorely tempted to reveal.

While many tenants were initially upset with us, they all in the end understood that we had done nothing malicious, thanks mainly to some brilliant face-to-face meetings done by our property manager, Rhonda. They all found alternatives, many with our help. A few, but not many, chose to stay with their new 'landlord'. Through a tricky period we had done the right thing, behaved appropriately according to our Values, upheld our reputation, and I am glad to say remained in contact with all our former tenants.

As a team we have decided never to work with this agent again, in any capacity.

This episode is one of many where the team share what has happened, and this process of sharing helps unite the team in a common understanding based around our Values.

My point is that in business no matter how much we try to control things, the truth is that much of what happens is outside of our control. When incidents such as I have just described happen to us we have a strong team that is flexible enough and innovative enough to be able to work their way through this and any situation. The strength of a business is not in what it does, but in how the team responds when things go wrong. And the behaviour for the team comes from a clear understanding of our Values and Purpose.

The culture slowly emerges and strengthens.

The flow // accommodating growth

Even back in my father's day we talked about how new business owners would start at home, then move into our business units. For them taking on their first lease would be an anxious time. We gave our support and good-natured enthusiasm for what they were doing. We noticed that many of them grew, and took larger premises on the Park. New units built in 1987 were for the growth of existing businesses, and that has been the process which has fuelled the growth of the Park.

As our customers succeed, so do we.

Of course, there comes a time when the businesses have grown so large that we can no longer accommodate them. At this time they have to choose to limit their growth and remain with us, or leave the Park in order to facilitate further growth. Those that leave take with them an understanding of how a commercial landlord can behave, and generally they have a more difficult time with their new landlords. And, of course, they move out of large premises, which leaves a big gap for us to fill. Medium-sized businesses that are already on the Park move in to the space made available, and young businesses fill up the space they vacate. This flow is a natural aspect of doing business our way, where change is embraced.

All pretty obvious, and emulated by many others, I am sure.

What I noticed, though, was a similar pattern happening with the team. The growth in question is not in terms of their size (despite numerous cakes!), no – it is to do with growth in self-confidence and self-belief, a direct result of the environment at Jennings which encourages team members to try something new and to take a risk. This is encapsulated in our Principle of 'Opportunities not Roles'. I am proud that every single member of the team (including me) has grown more confident while working with us. Some roles have expanded and grown as the company has grown, but in reality the number of roles is limited in a small company. In the end, this process of personal growth means that some team members are having to choose. If they stay with us they could limit their opportunities for future personal growth. If they leave they could expand beyond what we are able to offer. There is a potential for a flow of team members which is similar in construct to the flow of tenants.

I have encouraged one or two of the team to move on. Not because I want them to go – on the contrary they are all valued team members – but because I think they could personally grow further and faster elsewhere, and they could stagnate staying with us. It comes from care. As with our

177

larger tenants, when they leave they would leave a big hole that needs to be filled. By leaving they would give both themselves an opportunity to grow through a new experience somewhere else, and another team member an opportunity to try out the job vacated. They could also do such a great job teaching others about our Values and Purpose.

As yet, few have chosen to leave. I guess I am not really surprised. I have realised that the safety we provide as a business is very attractive so of course team members want to stay. The question then is not how to encourage them to move on, but how to retain their interest in Jennings, and how to build the business in such a way that we can all continue to grow. This is part of our challenge now.

This natural developmental flow is part of the culture, and something which we have come to understand and embrace.

Personal development and coaching // for all

One of my jobs as chairman, and one which is both challenging and a great pleasure, is team development. We have tried bringing in outside coaches, but quite honestly we have found that for the most part they learn more from us than we do from them. Many of them try to apply standard coaching processes on us, and we are well beyond that.

I have facilitated some discussions at team meetings, where we explore some of the concepts brought up in the Principles, such as what it means to challenge and how we give permission to each other to do just that. There is no structure to these meetings – we just play it by ear and explore together where they take us. The outcomes are collaborative and agreed by all team members.

Most recently the team have approached a couple of coaches who we can work with so that they can design half-day team programmes which have evolved from our Values and Principles.

I also meet up with the team members on a one-to-one basis every six months. This is not an appraisal; it is a meeting where I explain that in my view working at Jennings is not about what the employee can do for the company, but rather what the company can do for the employee. So the basic question is 'what do you want to do with your life, and how can we help you get there'. In a sense it is a way to explore their own individual sense of Purpose. Why are they here working with us? How does their own personal Purpose align with our business Purpose? These meetings are held in strict confidence so that the team members feel free to open up about their anxieties and fears. I neither talk about salaries, nor set them. I learn. And I hope they learn from me. Sometimes I feel that I have to be positive for them until such time as they can see it for themselves. So many of us see ourselves in a negative way. Sometimes by accentuating the positive, noticing initiative, and praising good work I can help them start to believe more in themselves and their contribution to the team. I use this time to enhance the good work of other team members, and sometimes to propose a different perspective when they are pulled down by uncertainty. It is a safe place to be open and honest. Often I talk from my experiences of mistakes and failures; we all make them, and of anxieties and worries. As stand-up comedian Simon Amstell says: 'People find it difficult to talk about the things they find embarrassing or shameful about themselves, and I think that is what I am up to: I'm exposing myself in order to make myself and the people in the room feel less alone.'

As the business culture matures I have noticed that other team members have coaching skills that they naturally apply, usually in a casual and caring way. This developing process is essential to a well-balanced team.

The senior team have now come up with the concept of Continuing Personal Development, or CPD. The idea being that each person in the team will be encouraged to work out a way in which they can commit to self-development, and the company will support them. For example, they may choose to take some paid time off to volunteer, or they may choose to use a personal coach. I am curious to know what ideas will come forward, and delighted that the team are evolving these methods.

John Strelecky has written an interesting book on this subject, *The Big Five for Life*. In it he insists that each employee must state five things they want to do before they die. They have to write these five things on the corridor wall for all to see. And then, as a company and as a team, they try to help make these things happen for every employee.

The lesson for other business owners is that we each have to find ways of showing our teams that we care for them, every one of them.

As our team has grown in confidence, so they have each learned to assess others on their behaviour. This means that everyone is constantly appraising everyone else. This can, of course, be by way of positive feedback such as praise, appreciation or gratitude. Or it may be something contrary to our Values and so the process would be noticing, tolerating, challenging if appropriate, and rejecting, again if appropriate. We can trust that all members of our team are capable of choosing new team members, new tenants or new contractors, and they are equally capable of rejecting them if they believe it is necessary.

More generally, I have a not-so-secret ambition that every single member of the team is capable of showing round a prospective tenant, explaining the lease terms and negotiating a fair price with them, and overseeing their moving in. This is a job that need not be reserved for professionals or managers. Any team member could do it as long as the managers are prepared to allow them the opportunity.

All this is made possible by the team understanding, accepting and embracing our Values and having a sense of common Purpose beyond maximising profit.

[

Good coffee and good service

A recent example is where a couple of the team decided to buy a coffee machine for the office. The choice they came up with was from a corporate business where the coffee was good, or a more local family business where the coffee was not so good. They noticed that the corporate was focused primarily on selling and the local firm focused primarily on service. In the end they decided not to go ahead until they could find a local company that focused on service that also had good coffee. Interestingly the price was a minor part of this discussion, but was not ignored. This was all done without managerial input.

]

Trust and generosity // the key to good business

It is no coincidence that the emerging culture is firmly based on trust coupled with the ability to be generous over and above the desire to maximise profit.

Trust is not something that comes easily to everyone; we all have to work at it. By extending trust to someone, we leave ourselves open to be taken advantage of. If there has been one, two or many episodes where people have taken advantage of your trust, then it is easy to put up barriers and learn never to trust anyone. This is especially so if there are childhood issues to do with abandonment, abuse or lack of love.

If we live our lives not trusting anyone, whatever the reason, then that serves only to prevent our growth. This is a situation where a great team can help. In any group where there is a strong sense of trust then, if encouraged and supported, each new team member can slowly learn to lower their natural barriers – the barriers that we learn to raise in order to prevent others from hurting us emotionally.

I have seen this happen many times. The team becomes a therapeutic community. In a recent team meeting we had no agenda except a check-in. The first person to speak talked about her child's anxiety attacks, and what she was doing about it. Her pain was clear. In opening up, she gave permission for others to do the same, and almost everyone briefly shared some current difficulties from their life. We all have them.

Generosity: an example from the mentoring service

One client, who is an agent, explained that he was having difficulty attracting new customers. I talked to him about the importance of building relationships, creating a network, and attracting people to him through his behaviour. A few weeks later he explained how he had been asked by another agent if he would do some work at no cost for one of her elderly clients. His initial reaction was to charge a fee for the service, but on reflection of our conversation decided not to charge. His little act of generosity resulted in a deeper connection with the other agent, and some collaborative contracts.

In contrast, it is relatively easy to be generous with company money or time. There are no heavy emotional consequences. Once generosity is allowed and even expected in a team, then it is a question of how the team member learns to balance generosity with the need to earn a profit. This balance is achieved through team discussion and learning from each other.

Through trust in each other, and the mindful application of generosity towards each other, the team at Jennings has become a very strong team. No one is protective of their role. No one is dependent on their role. Everyone recognises that other team members value them as a person, rather than as merely a doer of tasks. They have seen from the top down the ability to give away roles and look for other opportunities. They are positively encouraged to do the same. This can be done effectively if both parties to this transfer understand and adopt our Values, Purpose and Principles.

The advantage is that every member of the team grows in self-confidence and that opens up the opportunity for innovation at all levels in the business. Innovation leads to lowering costs, simplifying processes and improving services. This leads to growth in both size and profit of the business and that, in turn, creates further opportunities for the team. Business growth, then, is directly related to individual self-confidence.

I am not saying the transformation has been easy. People have wobbled in the face of change – that is why the one-to-ones have been so helpful. What I am saying is that those who have succeeded in facing their fears are now capable of understanding the process and in their turn helping others to do the same.

And so the culture emerges, strengthens and evolves.

I am not in charge of the culture.

I hope I have said enough in this chapter to show clearly that while the culture started from my sense of doing the right thing by valuing everyone, I am not in charge of the culture. My job has been to set the scene and then, with the team, develop a set of guidelines. Now my role is to step away and allow the team to develop the culture. This is happening in real time, and it is a joy to watch it evolve.

This process of letting go is crucial in any organisation, at all levels, and also one of the hardest things for a business owner to do. I am blessed that the team understand how hard it has been for me to let go of my baby (the culture I have nurtured for 20 years), and as a result they do involve me in the overview, but not the detail. For my part I get to watch from the side lines and marvel at how the team is developing the culture and therefore the business through consistent and diligent application of the Values, through purposeful decision-making and through their many and varied community connections.

CHAPTER TWELVE

The
Future

Building a legacy

We've built such a skilled team, they no longer need me.

Guy Watson –
Riverford Organic Farmers

I really love this quote from Guy Watson. It speaks of and from humility, perhaps the greatest and most admired attribute of a true leader.

The transition at Jennings has been from what I now realise is an increasingly outdated method of running a business primarily for short-term profit, to one where the objective is social in nature (and by that I include environmental), thus building a new paradigm.

It is a transition:

- from selfishness to selflessness,
- from self-service to service,
- from taking to sharing,
- from growth to sustainability,
- from possession to fulfilment,
- from anti-social to social,
- from poverty thinking to abundance thinking,
- from division to unity,
- from demarcation to innovation
- from control to trust,
- from heirarchy to equality,
- from management to leadership,
- from self-doubt to self-confidence;
- and, in summary, from fear to love.

In this emerging business culture, conduct is all important, for in my experience that is where sales come from and that is how a business grows. Treat people with respect and they will help you build your business by recommendation – marketing by attraction.

In this emerging culture, the Purpose of business is to put People before Profit. The business owner recognises that the desire for personal fulfilment is a pre-condition for ethical and moral success, which in turn leads to financial success.

In other words that the business-owner needs to:

- be able to understand the Purpose, for that is the source of fulfilment and motivation;
- have the courage to communicate the Purpose, to attract and lead other motivated people;
- be able to hold true to a clear set of personal Values;
- be prepared and able to uphold these concepts above the base desire to maximise profits above all else;
- be able, through shared Values and a common Purpose, to develop a united team, with each member retaining their individuality sufficiently to be person they want to be.

The team is then highly motivated and freed up sufficiently by the environment that has been established to be innovative in everything they do. And that leads to financial success.

A new way of doing business

Make no mistake: this cultural change is coming – and fast. Business has always been about building relationships, and now with the impact of social media it is harder for the abusers to hide. There is a growing sense of what is fair and what is unfair, what is real news and what is fake, unencumbered by press releases, and let loose by

Putting profit before people

A good example was of the BP oil spill in the Gulf of Mexico (from the *Deepwater Horizon*), after which BP tried to minimise the financial damage to the company rather than admit their mistakes and just deal with the problem. A similar situation has arisen with British Airways as they have been less than honest about the compensation passengers can claim for the delays caused by IT problems. BA put the company's profits before being fair to their customers.

whistle-blowers. Reputation is hard to gain and easily lost. Through social media, companies are not blamed for their failures but for their lack of transparency.

Everyone can accept failure, but strength of character is marked by how you deal with the failure, not the failure itself.

We are sometimes so bound up by the short-term loss that we fail to see the long-term impact. If 'Fairness' was a Value, and if 'Honesty' was a Value, these problems would be dealt with differently.

Who really feels comfortable working for companies that treat others in this way? The best people, the thinkers, those of independent mind, are beginning to choose to work for the more ethical companies.

The diligent consumer is careful nowadays to select ethically sourced, Fairtrade, local and/or organic products. There will be a tipping point where more people choose ethics over price.

One of the prominent inequities in the dying business culture is the disparity of executive salaries compared to the lowest or average salary in a business. It has been with us for years and is attaining political prominence now. I would like to see a well-publicised league table of the worst culprits, together with a list of brands that support the businesses that acquiesce to this greed. With adequate information, consumers can choose with their wallets.

Better-late-than-never generosity

One day, profit will be used as a force for good. Enterprise will not be about how much money you make, but rather how you made it and what you do with it. There is something inherently wrong with the business owner who makes so much money that he ends his life as a philanthropist, expecting us to be grateful for his guilt-driven, better-late-than-never generosity. It is far better, and increasingly common, for business owners to behave out of respect for others every single day, and to wisely use surplus profits as they arise.

And while we are on the subject of time-slipping generosity, there is also the issue of companies that are generous in some, but not in other areas of their business, depending on consumer expectation. So, for example, if a company is careful to be ethical with its sourcing of coffee beans because that is what consumers expect, that does not make it an ethical business if at the same time it is inconsiderate of the environment in water extraction and bottling.

Similarly, having exemplary after-sales service may well be part of a process of honouring customers, but that does not make a company ethical if at the same time it imposes 'gag' orders on its staff.

189

Simply stating that you are ethical does not make it so. Behaviour is what counts.

Being ethical is not a part-time activity, it is not a time-slip activity, and it is not a person-segregated activity.

A truly ethical enterprise starts with engagement from the top and trickles down through all aspects of the business.

Beyond Jennings

Over time, we as a team have begun to work only with customers and providers who share our Values. Over time, with the way we behave towards them, I have noticed that some of our customers and providers feel able to emulate our example. If our experience is one where people take from us, then we learn to take from others. And where our experience is more around people being generous and showing they care, then we can emulate that example.

As I have already stated, people respond positively when we extend trust, kindness, care and generosity. What also happens is that people learn those behaviours and start to treat others (their teams, their customers and their suppliers) in the same way. Generosity breeds generosity, kindness breeds kindness. I see this happening on our Business Park, and it is part of the reason why our strapline of 'a home for your business' comes to life.

In the UK there are millions of small businesses where the owners have started from a moral standpoint, with a sense of Purpose which motivates them to take risks, and with a sense of the freedom that comes with self-employment.

They get battered by business life. These business owners regularly suffer abuse from employees, from customers, from suppliers, from the public sector – all trying to take advantage. It is often subtle, but it has impact. Abuse crushes. It creates barriers and closes down through rule setting.

The story of Jennings describes an alternative. We can learn to tolerate, to forgive, to let go and to move on. A clear set of Values give us a platform for doing this. We can use authentic Values to call out bad behaviour or abuse. We can identify the abusers and challenge them. Once we know how to isolate the abusers, then we can create space for Values to play their part in a business.

The future?

That is not to say that the task at Jennings is complete. We know that in everything we do improvement is both possible and desirable. Our Value of Commitment is not to simply provide a service beyond expectation, but also to be able to continuously improve that service. The whole team can do that, and they do. Also our Principles of Change and Continual Improvement express this very well. Note that there is nothing in our Purpose, Values or Principles that states that we wish to change in order to make more money. On the contrary, change is for the sake of furthering our Purpose.

We also know that we are changing the world around us. By behaving with honour, and showing respect for all, we are leading the way for a behavioural change in business, starting from the small businesses and hopefully spreading to the larger ones.

Jennings is just one of many businesses which are exploring new cultures. It is worth reading a book called *Reinventing Organisations* by Frederick Laloux. This is a description of various companies' protocols using a colour theme. The old-school 'control and dominate' type of business being red, and the newer businesses, which adopt a more caring even spiritual approach are teal. As a social researcher, Laloux writes in some depth about how these companies behave, as well as the green and orange companies whose behaviour lies somewhere between. Jennings fits squarely into the teal bracket.

The examples he introduces are all larger organisations with many employees. What is interesting is that it always starts with the team, and that means that there needs to be a good leader. The problem is that no one teaches us how to be a leader. We have to work it out for ourselves. Authentic leaders are humble and have empathy, integrity and a strong sense of Purpose which they lead on. One of the main jobs of a leader is to support their followers. If you look after your team, then your team looks after the customers, and the customers look after the profit.

And finally, a message to all those reading this book who still think that a business cannot be operating effectively if it is not focused on profit.

Do not get confused. I am and have always been an advocate of my family business making profit. It is a 'for-profit' enterprise and all of the team know and accept that. What I am advocating, however, is that it is possible not only to make a profit but to actually improve profits by positively deciding to run your business for good. It is not so much about the amount of profit as it is about what you do with the profit you make.

Taking advantage of others, using your power over others, controlling people – these are all methods that can build profits in the short term, but in doing so we create stress and anxiety, dysfunction, dependency and victims. I would go as far as to say that the reason people use these techniques is for fear that if they don't, then something will go wrong and they may be blamed.

Growing a business through building relationships based on fairness and trust is admittedly not easy, but it is ultimately very rewarding and fulfilling. Business owners who do this are much happier people - vibrant and full of life, passionate and determined – and so are their teams. In the long run, these are the businesses of our future. The owner of the business has to work beyond his or her fear of failure, beyond the comfort of controlling others, and start to extend trust.

It is a difficult process to go through, but arguably the fear of embracing this culture is the one main reason why businesses remain small, or ultimately fail.

And finally

When you meet someone who owns their own business, take a moment to ask them *why* they do it – not *what* they do but *why* they do it. A response 'to earn a living' is, in my experience, a response designed to deflect the question. Ask again, and then be prepared to listen as the passion unfolds in front of you. These are the people who will build the future businesses and in doing so they will make a social and societal difference.

As socially aware business-owners, we know that that our message can easily be diluted, and each individual in our team has to recognise that we cannot give way to the forces that try to persuade us back to the profit motive. We notice:

- when our friends talk about how much they earn rather than how much they enjoy their job;
- when friends or family talk about material things rather than emotional or spiritual things;
- when people talk about how they have 'won' or gained from another, rather than when they have been generous or fair to another;

When people do these things and excuse it as 'well they would have done it to me' or 'it's just business'. Just because we can tread down on someone else does not mean to say that we have to do it.

On the other hand we also notice:

- when one of our friends says that they have been told to do something that they are not comfortable with, and we can help them with the emotions around that;
- when one of our friends talks about inequity in their community and we can help them with that;
- when one of our friends talks about how they have helped another person.

When we talk about the good stuff which we have learned from our culture, then that encourages people to talk about the good things that they have done. By being brave enough to talk about it, and by risking the unbalanced ridicule of some, we open up the possibility for authentic discussions around the better things in life – and our understanding of our Values helps us with clarity in these discussions.

Our message is important. With it we can challenge others, and effect change in the world.

'Never doubt that a small group of thoughtful, committed citizens can change the world; indeed, it's the only thing that ever has.' Margaret Mead, American anthropologist.

It is our duty to do whatever is in our power to help and support everyone who wants to run their business on this ethical, sustainable basis, and I hope this book goes a small way to doing just that.

APPENDIX

The
Principles

———

Expansion of the Principles

When reading these Principles, please be mindful of the overall intention, which is to move towards individual freedom and equality. If team members feel that they have freedom to make decisions on behalf of the company, and if they sense that they are treated as equally important in the team, then they are likely to show more commitment to the company and its leaders. This sounds rather grand, and requires some explanation.

Freedom

We are surrounded by controls – rules, regulations, processes, protocols, being taught how to behave, cultural norms. We are told what to do. We even control our own lives by conforming, or by taking the easy options. We become independent not when we break the rules of normality, but when we have something more important in our lives, perhaps a Purpose. Then we are prepared to innovate and sometimes break the rules for the sake of something more important. Then we dare to be different. The point is that we have choice.

At Jennings, as landlords, we have deliberately removed the controls around the lease so that all our tenants can vacate at short notice. They choose not to vacate, but they can if they need to. Our tenants are very independent people (entrepreneurs) and it is not wise to try to control them when that control is unnecessary. Allow them freedom, and then build a proper relationship. The vast majority of our tenants choose to stay. Tenants who grow too big for our Park can easily move on, and they keep us in the loop about their decision, making it easier for us to plan the next occupier of the building they vacate. We want to grow our business with tenants who want to stay with us, and not with those controlled by the lease leash.

In the same way, we want to help members of our team to become more independent and more self-reliant.

Freedom for our team is about making it possible for them to be able to make the choice to improve, to grow, to face fears in a trusting environment, and ultimately the choice to move on for the sake of their continual growth.

We create the environment to enable our team to take authority, as long as they behave responsibly and are accountable for their actions. The environment to which I refer is encompassed in our Purpose, Values and Principles.

A team is made up of many varied individuals. One way we can assess them is on a chart of dependency. The most dependent have the greatest fear of change and these employees will shy away from trying out new roles in case they make a mistake. They fear the unknown situation. They worry about what others think of them, and they people-please. The environment at Jennings is one of care, kindness, understanding, trust and encouragement which creates the opportunity and support for any team member to grow in self-confidence, and that is the beginning of them becoming independent. I can confidently say that every member of our team has grown in this way, and I can also say that observing their growth has for me been one of the most fulfilling aspects of running the business.

Incidentally, we also want our contractors to be free, in the sense that we want them to decide what to do in any given situation without having to ask. We expect them know what needs doing and just get on with it, rather than asking permission at every decision point. We also expect them, rather than merely doing what they are told, to be aware of up-to-date methods and apply their skills to deliver the best service. Our contractors have the authority to do this.

Why is this all important? Because when people we work with know that we trust them to do what is necessary, then we stop micro-managing and are free to focus on developing the business. Put another way, if we micro-managed every situation we would stifle the development and growth of the business.

Equality

We recognise that every team member has an equal opportunity to improve and to contribute. We are equally able to care about each other, be kind to each other and encourage each other. We choose not to use any power we may have over other team members, customers or suppliers, or anyone else for that matter.

We put our Purpose above all else — to create an environment where people feel valued.

The basis for that comes from a belief that we are all equals and we can all value each other equally. In most organisations we see only inequality, because we look only at the hierarchical structure, the salary or other material things. That is why it is important to focus on other aspects of relationships that make us feel equally valued as a team member.

Equality also spreads to how we treat other people and allows us to set limits on the behaviour that we accept from others before we challenge them. We do not allow others to exert their power over us.

We consider ourselves equal to all others, and importantly that others are equal to us, for without that we could not deliver our Purpose.

As you read through each of the Principles please think about how it reflects back on freedom and equality.

Principles relating to working as a team

Unity — putting the team first

Support and respect for each other is the key to upholding our Purpose.

If we are to create 'an environment where people feel valued', then the place to start is at the heart — with the team.

We are each responsible for building this environment in our workplace and we do this primarily by focusing on the Values. They give us a useful template for behaviour towards each other.

A united team is a joy to behold. The team itself represents the company. That is why behaviour is so important. A united team is one where every person understands each other.

Unity comes from acceptance of and adherence to our Purpose and Values.

If a team member feels they cannot uphold the Purpose, then it is time for them to leave. Team members leave with our blessings and our good wishes for the next part of their journey. We hope they will have learned enough with us to be able to practise some of our Principles in their new place of work.

When we recruit, we take care to give plenty of time for the incoming team member to become used to our culture. It is essential that we build unity as we grow the team, and we have to be particularly aware of those who join the team where the old methods are so ingrained that they cannot adapt to our emerging culture. We have to be diligent. Not all new recruits complete our three-month induction period.

Service and Gratitude

We are a service-orientated company. While financiers and tax authorities may view us as a property investment company, our true calling is in our service to our tenants. Our financial investment is in bricks and mortar, but our authentic or emotional investment as a team is in our commitment to serve our tenants. Being of service also applies to each other in the team and, of course, to our suppliers and the outside community.

It is important to distinguish between service and servitude. We are not slaves to the company, nor to any one individual.

We do what we do because we are motivated to do it, because we enjoy being of service, because serving others is fulfilling.

When we serve each other we are prepared to help and support where a team member is struggling. There is never an occasion where one team member can say 'I will not help because it is not my job'. It is particularly important that our leaders always remember that a key part of their job is to serve the team. Too often leaders think their job is to manage, and that turns the team members into servants, while a 'worthy leader has a desire to serve, not dominate' (*Autobiography of a Yogi* by Pramahansa Yogananda). A leader's job is to uphold the Purpose and create an environment in which the team can flourish.

We serve our suppliers by respecting and valuing their opinion, expecting that they will give us great service (just as we give great service to our customers), and by paying their invoices promptly.

We serve our community by consulting with them, by getting involved, by supporting local charities, events and individuals, and by being available if we are asked.

The other side of service is gratitude for a service received.

Gratitude is often under-rated, and especially so when what you do is considered to be 'just doing your job'. Service beyond expectation, or going that extra distance, shows commitment and will often earn praise and gratitude.

Gratitude is more important than gratuity.

Gratuity turns great service into a contract whereas gratitude turns great service into a relationship.

As a team we can practise gratitude for each other.

It is very important when you receive gratitude to accept it. So many people turn it down, by for example dismissing the event as 'nothing special'. Be aware that this response is like a slap in the face to the gratitude giver. It is their gratitude, not yours.

Accept gratitude as a gift; accept it with grace.

Great service is essential in building trusting relationships, and being able to accept gratitude as the gift that it is helps to grow personal self-confidence.

Authority and Responsibility

Our stated Purpose and our Values give each team member a safe platform for making decisions without needing to refer to a manager. We aspire to give authority to every member of the team to take it upon themselves to do the right thing, for the right reason. Actually it is more than that. We do not 'give' authority, as that starts with the assumption that it is ours to give, and that is limiting. Instead we create the environment where team members feel comfortable to assume authority– the one proviso being that they must also honour the responsibility and accountability which comes with authority.

Taking responsibility has a number of effects.

1 It is one of the first ways in which a person can build their self-confidence and self-esteem. We provide a safe environment where team members can do that. One of the greatest pleasures running a small business is to watch team members grow from timidity to confidence – and that process happens, and is happening to all of us.

2 It requires being accountable for your actions. Being honest about what you have done after the event. Whether the action was correct or incorrect or could have been better, can be discussed at team meetings so that it becomes a point of learning for all team members.

3 Failure must be embraced, and accepted as a part of this process. *Without acceptance around failure no one would take responsibility – for fear of reprisal.* We all make mistakes. We need to laugh at mistakes so that everyone has permission to make them, and so that everyone is comfortable taking responsibility. The fear of reprisal is one of the biggest problems in British business today. Much innovation and creativity is stifled for fear of failure, because failure can lead to blame, judgement and thence to reduced bonus, poor appraisals, and reduced career prospects. It is no wonder that in most corporates and bureaucracies employees tend to do only what they are told to do.

The greatest leaders:
- accept their mistakes without trying to lay blame;
- are happy to communicate their mistakes;
- accept that this makes them vulnerable, but also understand that this makes them accessible;
- make it acceptable for everyone in the team to embrace failure as a point of learning.

Fail once, but don't keep failing — learn, and teach.

4   It frees up others to do their own jobs. If no one took responsibility, then everything lands on the desk of the manager, who will spend all his/her time micro-managing at the expense of other work which could enhance the business.

This is both a slow process and a continual process. Every team member is becoming more self-confident, and learning to be more self-reliant through this process. Each time we learn something new, our confidence grows. As we gain experience so we can become a teacher for someone else. Having taken responsibility for a task, we can then pass the authority on to someone else so that they can take responsibility.

In this process of accepting a task, facing your fears, embracing failure, completing the task, and then letting go of it to someone else we embrace the idea that change is good, even exciting. Our team members look forward to the next challenge.

Equality

If we do not consider ourselves as equal, then by default we must consider ourselves either better or less than another person. In our team we focus on the similarities which make us equal, and the differences that make us not better, but unique. Every team member is expected to take action to help another feel less subservient and more of service.

You will see that equality is bound up in most of the Principles.

Challenging

So often we shy away from challenging another person for their actions or behaviour. We think that we may upset them. We think that they may receive a challenge as criticism. Often we get so wound up by the behaviour of another person that our challenge blurts out and will indeed come across as critical.

In the Jennings team we agree to accept challenges as a normal part of our day. We recognise that when we are being challenged by another member of the team, it is because that person wants to help us, and recognises something in us, or some behaviour, that we do not see ourselves.

A useful platform for challenging behaviour is when we can recognise behaviour that is contrary to our Values. For example if a team member is not making someone feel at home, or could do more or better work to make someone feel at home. The recipient, being open-minded, learns new ways, and the challenger learns better how to get their message across.

By giving ourselves permission to be challenged we learn and we improve, and steadily a good team becomes a great team. By giving ourselves permission to be challenged by any member of the team, no matter their perceived status, brings equality in to the team. I like it when team members challenge me – it means that they are comfortable with me – the relationship is sound.

As we practise this process in the team, so we have less fear in challenging outside of the team. We begin to challenge tenants who for example may not be fair with us. We begin to challenge providers who give a poor service (for example if a contractor is disrespectful of our tenants).

Over time our standards have improved. We expect our providers nowadays to do more than provide a basic service, we expect them to understand us, care about us, and provide a service beyond our expectation. If we can do it for our customers, we want to be recipients of similar service. Our standards are high, and we expect high standards from the people we work with.

Providers who do not respond to our challenges, who are not willing to adapt when we gently remind them of their behaviour, will not get further work with us.

Incidentally it is a leadership quality to challenge someone else.

Be a leader. Challenge when you see an action or behaviour that could be improved, and do not be attached to the response, for you cannot and must not control or be controlled by the response.

Communication

As we have seen with our Value, Openness and Honesty are essential factors in minimising fears and anxieties. Of course this also works within the team. Honesty and Openness lead to trust. If I only talk about my successes the team members will begin to doubt me, if I also admit to my failures the team begin to trust that I am telling the whole truth. This is why humility is an essential attribute of an authentic leader. A humble leader will openly admit his or her mistakes, and an arrogant leader will hide them.

When we admit our failings, we face our fear that other team members may judge us, but in a strong team, where behaviour is based on Values, we learn that admitting our failings is a relief. The guilt and the sense of being less than the next person falls away. We also learn that we are still accepted by the team, that the team can all learn from our failures, that everyone in the team makes mistakes because that's human.

At Jennings, we have regular team meetings where we share information about what is happening at work, and sometimes more personal things. An initial 'check-in' to see how we are grounds the meeting and allows everyone to clear any anxieties. All meetings are important ways of building channels of communication in which our Purpose and Values can be upheld, and to build a sense of all being 'in it together'. But this only works if all members of the team are prepared to be completely honest with each other.

Opportunities, not roles

In business we have become used to, and we now accept, that taking on a new employee is a contractual arrangement. A person is told what to do, and then paid the going rate as compensation for their time. Swathes of Human Resources issues have led businesses to compound this process by issuing extensive employment contract documents – covering all sorts of things from hours to health and safety rules – and their main purpose seems to be to limit any possibility of the employer being at fault if something goes wrong.

Of course we have to comply with legislation, and so much of the documentation is necessary – though we try to write ours in understandable English!

At Jennings, our focus is not on the job our employees do, but on the opportunities we can present to them. We do not want any members of our team to be constrained by their role, we want them to be free to try new things, to stretch themselves. We understand that fears and anxieties hold us back, so we encourage all team members to face those fears and anxieties. We do this by giving team members the opportunity to do things they have not done before.

Done responsibly, with care and encouragement, we have had amazing success in transforming people's lives. We help every team member to become more confident, and their self-esteem steadily grows.

Team members recognise when one member has pushed themselves. We can see and feel the emotions: and whether the process was a success or failure, we can all appreciate that she has tried.

Furthermore the recognition that they are being cared about is highly motivating. Team members become extraordinarily committed to their current role in the clear knowledge that they will be able to pass it on to someone else as they progress, if they wish to.

This is a long process which gently unfolds, and in my view business owners have a responsibility to help their employees to become more confident and more self-reliant. Team members then become more effective and more able to work independently, taking action without asking first. This is a transition from dependency – only doing what they are told to do – to independency – just getting on with what needs doing.

To present an employee with opportunities means that the business owners and managers have to be very flexible and adaptable. This is a great discipline as it prepares us for change.

Change

People like things to remain the same. We get comfortable, like a pair of old slippers.

Same job, same commute to work, same home, same everything. (I once heard someone say that they were looking forward to going home for dinner because Tuesday night is lamb chops…)

When something changes, it unsettles us; we look for someone to blame or someone to show us what to do.

Rules and regulations are good because they guide us in what to do. We like rules, especially if they stay the same. We know where we are with rules, we know what to do. Professionals work with rules.

We like being told what to do by someone else: a parent, a school teacher, a manager. We are safe if we only do what we are told to do. Control is good, bureaucracy is good.

We cannot be wrong and we cannot make a fool of ourselves if we only do as we are told and stick to the rules.

Change is bad. Change means we have to respond and we may not have a manager or a regulation to tell us what to do.

Unfortunately none of the above is realistic. 'The only real constant in life is change' (Napoleon Hill, *Outwitting the Devil*). We think we can keep things the same, we can try to control things, and people, in order to keep things the same, but in the end change happens to us, and then eventually we realise that we are powerless.

We always have been powerless, and we always will be.

So the antidote to this is to embrace change. Accept it, be adaptable and adjust. In a business environment we can only do that if we understand why we are all in it together, how we have collectively agreed to behave: Purpose and Values. Then we can be responsible for any action we may take and any change that we make.

Entrepreneurs do not just embrace change, they are excited by change; they love it. Not all business owners are entrepreneurial, and it is important to recognise that the difference between an entrepreneur and a business owner lies in their ability to adapt to change, and in their ability to make change happen.

Entrepreneurs get bored very easily. If their business has grown, and done well financially, and is churning out the product or service comfortably and regularly, then entrepreneurs get twitchy, and they start to look at better ways, cheaper ways, easier ways to do things.

Entrepreneurs therefore are innovators.

In the Jennings team, we encourage everyone to be entrepreneurial. You do not have to run a business to be entrepreneurial – it is a state of mind. You do have to be comfortable with making mistakes, hopefully not big ones. If you are not making mistakes occasionally, then you are not trying hard enough – you are too comfortable. So every team member has a chance to innovate, and that is another way in which we accept that we are equals.

Control is the enemy of innovation. Ease up on control or micro-managing, begin to trust your team, then watch the business fly.

Continual Improvement

A form of control is the belief that there is perfection. 'My way is the only way.' 'Do as you are told.' At Jennings, we reject the idea that anyone or anything is perfect. Instead we have the attitude that everything can be improved.

Everything we do can and should be continually checked against 'is there a better way?' and 'do I even need to do this any more?' For everyone in the team to be able to do this, they must embrace the Purpose and Values to give themselves a baseline for change.

Everybody in the team has an equal ability to think for themselves. This is a freedom that is precious in business. Precious in the sense that it helps the individual on their road to self-confidence, and for the business in the sense that we keep ahead of the competition. In so many businesses people are not expected to think. They are expected to be automatons. This is such a waste of a huge resource that it is a tragedy. We do not have to be like that. Treat your team well and encourage them to think for themselves.

Values before qualifications

The old method of recruiting someone is to specify the role, and then expect that those who apply would show how they are capable of performing the role. A typical CV would show qualifications and experience. Questions asked by recruitment agencies, or by interviewers would generally be related to experience and whether a person can do the job. Salary negotiations are often a competitive process where an applicant who knows their value to the Company would ask for a higher salary. My point is that the whole process revolves around showing an ability to do the job. Questions beyond that tend to be limited to such as 'why do you want to join the company?'

Happily this is changing. More companies are recognising the need for a new member to 'fit' in with the team and to positively contribute, and so there are attitudinal questions at interviews as well as ability questions.

At Jennings, while the ability to do the job is important, the ability to fit with the team *takes priority*. For two reasons:

1 Firstly the particular role they have applied for is transitory in that we would invite the applicant to progress beyond that role, and

2 Secondly the applicant must share our Values so that they are more likely to fit in with the team.

We are interested in a person who is committed to service, honest and trustworthy, and courteous. Openness can often be determined by how chatty a person is at the interview, or in reception while waiting. Our receptionists' views are taken into account as part of the assessment of an applicant – was the applicant courteous, curious, easy-going, interesting?

Above all we look for people who are keen to adapt to change, and who are excited by the opportunity to learn on the job so that they can progress. We also expect them to be of service to the team they have joined. We do not want on our team anyone who thinks they are 'better' than the next person, whether that be because of position or qualification. There is no room for ego.

Also we have found that prior experience can be a problem in that a person can have pre-conceived methods that simply do not apply in our Company. This is why we have never recruited anyone with experience in the property industry – they tend to believe that their job should be focused on the property, whereas we operate with the knowledge that our investment is in our relationship with others. It is fundamentally different.

The second set of Principles relate to Purpose – and how we build relationships with others

Our Purpose is our ultimate authority

Our Purpose is *'To build an environment where people feel valued'*.

Our Purpose is not therefore to make money, our Purpose is what motivates us and what unites us as a team. Making a profit is an outcome of delivering our Purpose. Profit is reinvested in the Purpose.

If no Purpose is specified, then members of the team would default to assuming that our objective is to maximise profit. Similarly our customers and suppliers and the outside community round us would assume the same. Purpose gives us an alternative objective.

That is not to say that making a profit is not important. It is imperative that we generate a return on our investments. The business has to be financially sustainable in order to survive. Part of the responsibility of the team is to be keen on costs, and to be aware of what our prices should be in the marketplace. Fairness is important. It is just that if we did not state an alternative Purpose, then it would not be unreasonable for team members to be careless around costs, and to use their power to force higher rents for short-term gain, but at the expense of long-term relationships – and therefore long-term profits.

It is not the making of profit that is the problem, it is how you *behave* in order to make the profit, and how you *use* the profit.

We believe that profit can be made and utilised in a way that is both fair and not greedy or self-serving. While many people think this is unusual, it is our view that more and more business owners are thinking this way, and it is those people that we choose to work with.

On a daily basis, every decision made and every action taken by every member of the team is aligned to Purpose. Normally this happens naturally and sometimes, where a team member has been indecisive, it is good to remind them to go back to the basics – will your decision help to make people feel valued?

We want our team members to feel good when they have treated someone fairly without the worry that any minor loss of income to the Company may impact on their bonus or career prospects. Each team member is encouraged to challenge another where decisions or actions are not in line with Purpose. We all serve the Purpose.

Empathy, Courtesy, Generosity and Kindness

Understanding other people and the kindness we show them, particularly when they are in trouble, is a key to expressing our Purpose. We do this without judgement or expectation of return. Kindness is not a contractual obligation but a gift given freely.

For example, when a tenant has a cash-flow problem we hope that they trust us enough to inform us so that we can seek to understand their problem, and do whatever we can to help them through a bad patch. Even if the tenant simply does not pay, our response is to make a visit, and try to understand. This approach comes from the empathetic understanding that some tenants will not tell us that they cannot pay for fear that we may react badly, and it is our job to reduce the fear, not magnify it. Sometimes we will agree to give a rent-free holiday, sometimes a rent reduction, and usually some months later the debt will be repaid, and with appreciation. Thus we turn a difficult situation into one which builds the relationship.

The private lives of team members sometimes impact on their working life. Equally the working lives of some impact on their family. Where there is change at work, so that can manifest in the home. Where there are problems at home, that can manifest at work. We need to be mindful of these issues and try to understand and support those affected by them. We would hope that other team members would do the same for us, for none of us is immune from these problems, but many of us are good at pretending they do not exist.

There is never a situation where we would drop our commitment to courtesy. Courtesy makes another person feel valued and is therefore central to our Purpose.

Everything we think, say and do helps to build an environment where people feel valued. The environment is not just the physical environment, but how people feel about how they are treated. Thus by treating people with courtesy we show them that we care about them. This is not just a case of opening a door for someone. This is about understanding their needs and doing what we can to help them.

- Having a lease of only four pages, and written in plain English, is courtesy.

- Making sure there are enough car parking spaces on the Park is courtesy.

- Being welcoming to all guests is courtesy.

- Making sure that shared facilities are clean is courtesy.

Generosity comes about where we do not expect anything in return for the things that we do for others. We do it because it is the right thing to do, not because we will get some reward for it. Reward converts an act of generosity into a contract. A reward takes away the gift.

We can be generous in many ways and not just in relation to material things. We can be generous with the trust that we extend to others. We can be generous with appreciation for what someone has done. We can be generous in our gratitude. We can be generous with kind words, or with positivity, or with our acceptance of errors. Every team member is equally able to be generous.

We build community with others by being kind and caring. We do it for no other reason than it makes us feel good. We try to be kind to each other in the team, to our customers and to their teams, to our suppliers and their teams and to the outside community. We serve all of these people in everything we do and we care about each other. We give time to our tenants – when we go to see them there is no time limit on the conversation. Our team are encouraged to take a break for a free coffee (on our tab) at the café on the Park because by being there they will meet and communicate with tenants. There is no end to the inventiveness in ways in which we can be kind and caring to others, and the joy is that every member of the team can do that.

Building trusting relationships

Relationships are a two-way process. Of course, we can be kind, generous trusting, courteous and empathetic. But we cannot do this without limit We have boundaries. Boundaries are evolved from our Values. Where we are accommodating, we expect others to be accommodating towards us where we are trusting, we expect others to trust us; where we are fair, we expect others to be fair with us – and so on.

We first *notice* when someone does not respond to the way we treat them. Then we seek to *understand* why. We realise that often people have anxieties, or they put on a mask of self-confidence when really they are uncertain. There is a difference between that and someone who has a strong sense of their own self-importance, or who does things which are self-serving. We learn to spot these traits and that helps us to evaluate a prospective job applicant, tenant, supplier or contractor.

We have learned from experience that some people put themselves above the desire to build an equal relationship, and these people we choose not to work with.

Our culture comes from our sense of the importance of Values in building trusting relationships and this we hold as one of the most important factors in running our business. If someone's personality does not fit with our culture, then they are not welcome, and all of the team are empowered to deal with such people, and they all do, in their own way. This may sound a little harsh, but we have learned to be diligent around protecting our culture from those who unconsciously do things to undermine it.

We don't always get this right. It is a work in progress, a work of continual improvement.

The third set of Principles relate to Community

Marketing is by attraction rather than by promotion

Whether we like it or not, our brand is an extension of our culture, and our culture is an extension of how we behave towards others. When we treat customers well, then they will be likely to stay. That is why we have the Values of Commitment *for the sake of delivering a service beyond expectation*, and Fairness *for the sake of building loyalty and trust*. Some of those customers will recommend us to friends and recommendation, or 'word of mouth', is perhaps the best way to grow a sustainable business. Attracting customers through recommendation has the added advantage that we are more likely to attract the right kind of customers. It makes no sense in business to have awkward customers. If we have a scattergun approach to marketing – for example, by untargeted promotional activity – then we are more likely to be faced with awkward customers.

While customers attract customers, so employees attract employees and suppliers attract other suppliers – all by recommendation. This is how most small businesses grow. Furthermore we find that employees and suppliers attract customers, customers recommend people to be employees and suppliers and so on.

Jennings tenants are free to leave whenever they want to – we do not seek to control them through a long lease. They leave for all sorts of reasons; for example they may outgrow the Business Park, they may have found other premises closer to where most of their team live, they may have been taken over by another company, they may have gone into liquidation. No matter what the reason, we do not seek to hold them. We emphasise this to our team by understanding that each business that leaves the Park is an addition to our external marketing department. And we have indeed had recommendations from tenants who have left, sometimes many years later. This is also true of employees who have left.

Build a culture of respect for others, and the karmic effects kick in – people start to recommend your services.

It is, of course, accepted that this process is not fast. It takes time to build a reputation and for people to genuinely believe in you enough to recommend you. Most people are very careful when making recommendations as their own reputation is at stake. You would not recommend someone who gave you a bad service, and even if they gave a good service you would want to know that you could rely on them to provide an equally good service to the friend to whom you have recommended them.

Some business owners want to grow their business faster, and sometimes the business model requires fast growth to take advantage of a time-niche of the product/service. In that case promotional marketing is necessary – but that does not mean that reputation is not important.

At Jennings we have learned that it is very difficult to promote commercial property for rent. People tend to buy on price and location, and they are only interested when they have a need. It is therefore a bit pointless and a waste of money promoting any properties we have for rent in the local papers. Similarly we do not like to put 'To Let' signs up on our properties as it adds nothing to the environment in which others have to work. To-let signs on a business park are an expression of a landlord who puts profit before people; the advert for the landlord is more important than the environment for the tenant.

So we rely on people to come to us, and we work hard at attracting them to us, and also making sure we do nothing to put them off. This is in stark contrast to the majority of other business-park owners who actively promote through agents and newspaper advertising.

Social media is an excellent opportunity to show *how* we operate/ behave, as opposed to *what* we have available to rent, which, of course, is marketing by promotion. We do not attempt to control content of social media. We trust all of our team members if they are active on social media, recognising that each person's voice adds to the brand image.

Social media is in the hands of many people, therefore it is likely to be a more honest expression of who you are than a leaflet or TV advert which are designed to influence. It is hard to control social media, and inequity is easily exposed. This makes it a useful media for honest businesses to attract people to them.

Facilities and behaviour

The way we, that is all members of our team, behave to others, and the facilities we offer are in reality just an extension of our marketing by attraction. Behaviour and facilities are part of our brand. Everything sparks from respect for and of others. The Values form the basis for our behaviour, and we continually check in with each other that we are working to the Values. Our Values also form the basis for how we conduct our business, what we choose to do and not to do, and how we set prices.

Our strapline is 'a home for your business', but how can we make people feel at home when they are working with us? For me one of the nicest sentiments I hear from anyone visiting the Park is how relaxed, comfortable, safe, and calm they feel when they drive in. That is what makes my heart sing and glow with pride. And that is not an accident.

- We keep the place clean and tidy, but the tarmac is a bit pitted.
- We provide enough parking spaces so that no one needs to park on the road and block the traffic, but no parking spaces are reserved for any unit or individual.
- We keep the grass cut, but don't be surprised to see some weeds lurking in the shrubberies.
- We provide security, but not so much as to inconvenience our tenants, their staff and visitors.

In our serviced office building, the facilities are equally clean and tidy, but we have the added benefit of really good receptionists who are interested in whoever walks through the door, and I have seen them as comfortable teasing government ministers as they are delivery drivers.

As I write this, even last night I met someone who had just started working for a tenant in our office building and she was gushing over how amazing our toilets are! One thing I learned very early on in a serviced office environment is to make sure the toilets are presentable and clean.

There is no grandeur in our facilities or in our behaviour, and we all reject grandiose behaviour towards us as well. To be in service is not to be in servitude. We accept praise and gratitude, but that does not mean we are in some way better than another person, rather I would say that we lead the way as an example for others to follow if they choose.

Endorsement

We believe in the importance of building relationships. Proper relationships are built on trust.

People trust those with integrity, in other words what they think, say and do are one and the same.

Our Values give us a stable platform for building long-term relationships and we must do everything to strengthen those relationships, and nothing to damage them.

We notice that people around us try to get our endorsement of their products or services. It is really important not to be associated with people whose Values conflict with ours, as we would be giving out a message which undermines our Values and Purpose, and that will weaken our message.

A recommendation is a gift which comes with an understanding that the person recommended upholds our Values. We only recommend people we have a strong relationship with, who we can rely on to uphold the value of the recommendation. We cannot always get this right, but we can learn by getting feedback from the recipient as to whether a good service was provided. Note this has nothing to do with price, and everything to do with care.

When we sponsor an event, we are adding the unique marker of our Values to the event. This is not something we do deliberately, but we must be aware that when people see the Jennings brand as a sponsor or a participant, they will assume we endorse the event. We have certainly made mistakes in this area and endorsed people or concepts we should never have been party to. We are wiser now.

When we put on seminars or invite speakers, we are endorsing the speaker in front of an audience invited by us and who come to us because of what we stand for. We must honour the fact that the audience have given their time for us, and make sure that we put on seminars where the speaker gives great informative or entertaining talks, is not promoting themselves, and helps us to build relationships with the audience. The speaker comes as a volunteer and we hope that they are good enough that some of the audience may be attracted to work with them. We are endorsing the speaker and they benefit from that.

We never blanket recommend (for example, by mailshot or newsletter advert) or endorse any professional or other services to our tenants. It is too easy for our tenants to be suspicious that we may be profiting from the recommendation, and just that thought could dent our relationship, which is based on trust.

Grants and offers

We will not seek out grants for capital works, tax avoidance schemes or any other gifts as a team, or as an individual through working in the team, because they come with attachments and complications that can divert us from our Purpose. They take away our freedom.

We think that what we are getting is easy money. We think we may as well take it since it is on offer. Our experience has been that grants are generally not worth the hassle.

1 The public sector (where most grants emanate) is so highly audited that every aspect of the grant must be right and it is so easy to think you comply with all the conditions only to find at the last minute that your application is rejected for some minor point.

2 You can be treated really badly, with disdain even. The grant-givers tend to think that since it is free money, you would, of course, make the effort to make an application. They do not consider the opportunity cost of the time spent applying for grants.

3 The officers hold the purse to the cash and sometimes wield this power because they think you are dependent on them.

And quite apart from these points, which do not apply in all cases, the main issue is that the purpose of the grant will probably not coincide with your Purpose, and so the lure of the money diverts attention away from the reason you set the business up. This issue is particularly prevalent in charities, but applies also to businesses.

The point is not to refuse a grant, but rather to be aware that grant money does come with strings attached and you need to be very clear about the purpose of the grant and whether it aligns with your Purpose.

Tax avoidance schemes similarly divert attention from the main purpose of the business. Often these can be complex, and for small businesses any savings are often far outweighed by the costs in time, complication and an uneasy feeling that something is not quite right about the morality of the scheme. I remember our accountant of nearly

50 years service who used to say that paying tax is a sign of profitable business. Don't avoid tax, pay your dues. One day businesses that avoid tax through legal loopholes will be condemned.

We do, of course, accept gifts, especially at Christmas, where they are an expression of gratitude. For example, wine from our customers or hampers from our contractors. These are normally split among the team as the reason for the gift is due to a team effort and not in the remit of one team member.

The Jennings' message

Our message to all other people is that in business it is possible to put People before Profit. This message is encapsulated by our Purpose, Values and Principles, and indeed is the purpose of this book.

A strong team gives us the confidence to spread this message to anyone prepared to listen, for we believe that by living this culture we are giving others permission to adopt the same. We have found that 'it works if you work it'.

Our message takes courage to deliver in a business environment where most others assume the profit motive, and yet we are beginning to find more and more customers and suppliers who thrive on trusting us as much as we do by trusting them. We are building a business community around us of like-minded individuals who understand that fulfilment comes from serving others, not from greed, and we hope that as we grow that community and as we develop the community confidence, that we can spread the word about running a business for the good of everyone and not just solely for the benefit of the owners.